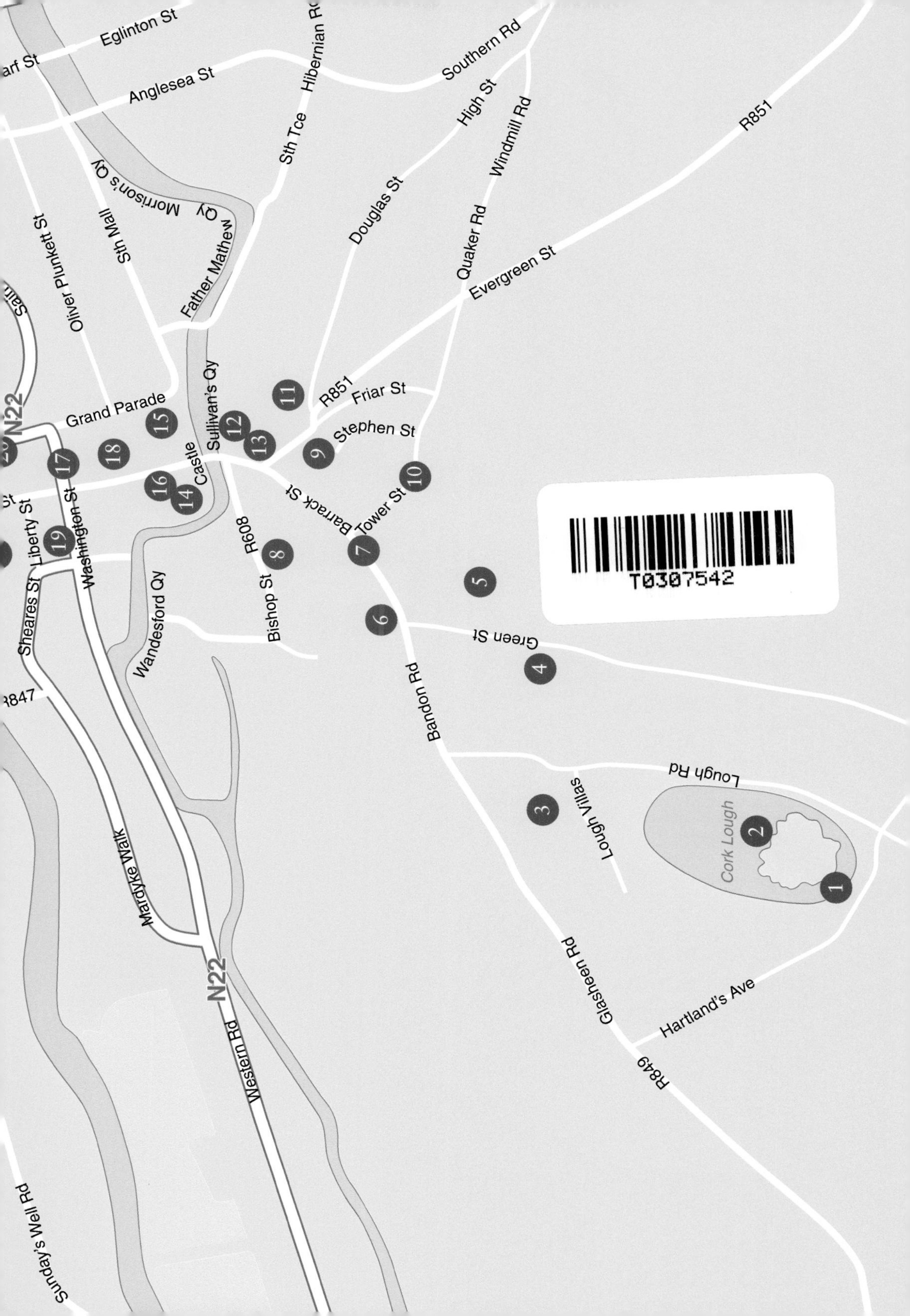

Eglinton St
Anglesea St
Southern Rd
Hibernian Rd
Sth Tce
High St
Windmill Rd
R851
Douglas St
Quaker Rd
Evergreen St
Morrison's Qy
Father Mathew Qy
Sth Mall
Oliver Plunkett St
N22
Grand Parade
Sullivan's Qy
Castle St
Friar St
R851
Stephen St
Barrack St
Tower St
Washington St
Liberty St
R608
Bishop St
Wandesford Qy
Sheares St
Green St
Bandon Rd
R847
Lough Rd
Lough Villas
Cork Lough
Mardyke Walk
N22
Western Rd
Glasheen Rd
Hartland's Ave
R849
Sunday's Well Rd
1
2
3
4
5
6
7
8
9
10
11
12
13
14
15
16
17
18
19

Introduction

Places matter in Cork. The city's urban landscape is filled with stories about its past, with some sites you might stop and contemplate as you're passing by, and many others you might not give a second look. But a second and even a third look can reveal some interesting historical nuggets and curiosities about Cork's development. In Cork it always pays to look above the ground floor to shop and house level.

From its marshy foundations at the lowest crossing point of the River Lee, the city spread across its steep suburban hillsides. This book is a cross-sectional journey from the south of the city to its northern prospects, commenting on a rich range of historic spaces, streets and laneways. The book is a walking trail, which can be physically pursued or you can simply follow it from your armchair.

Cork: A Potted History builds upon my other Amberley publication, *Secret Cork*, but this time it takes the viewer on a walking trail of over forty sites. It takes a line from the city's famous natural lake known just as The Lough across the former medieval core, ending in the historic north suburbs of Blackpool. Starting at The Lough – a Cork gem – which once hosted everything from duels to ice skating and its own tree nursery, the trail then rambles to hidden moats, ancient hospital sites, lost meeting houses, legacies of medieval remnants, across ancient streetscapes to forgotten industrial urban spaces. The book reveals the city's lesser-known heritage and hidden urban and cultural features. Enjoy.

CORK

A POTTED HISTORY

KIERAN McCARTHY

AMBERLEY

Dedicated to my nephew, John Michael.
Never forgotten, RIP.

First published 2024

Amberley Publishing
The Hill, Stroud
Gloucestershire, GL5 4EP

www.amberley-books.com

ISBN 978 1 3981 1431 9 (print)
ISBN 978 1 3981 1432 6 (ebook)

British Library Cataloguing in Publication Data.
A catalogue record for this book is available from the British Library.

Typesetting by SJmagic DESIGN SERVICES, India.
Printed in Great Britain.

I

The Heritage of The Lough

The Lough is one the city's key amenities, attracting people from across the city. Many local historians like Richard Henchion and Declan Myers have written on this district, as well as areas such as Glasheen, Ballyphehane and Togher. This 18-acre freshwater lake was created by the erosion of moving ice during one of the glacial periods, sometime between 10,000 and 2 million years ago. It rests on a bed of limestone running east and west about 60 feet above sea level.

It is the natural collection basin into which the higher encircling ground is drained. It is also fed by rainwater and by five subterranean streams. The glaciation erosion exposed the underling limestone, an easily dissolvable rock, and the action of the water congealed and became like cement, stopping further water from seeping through the rock cavities

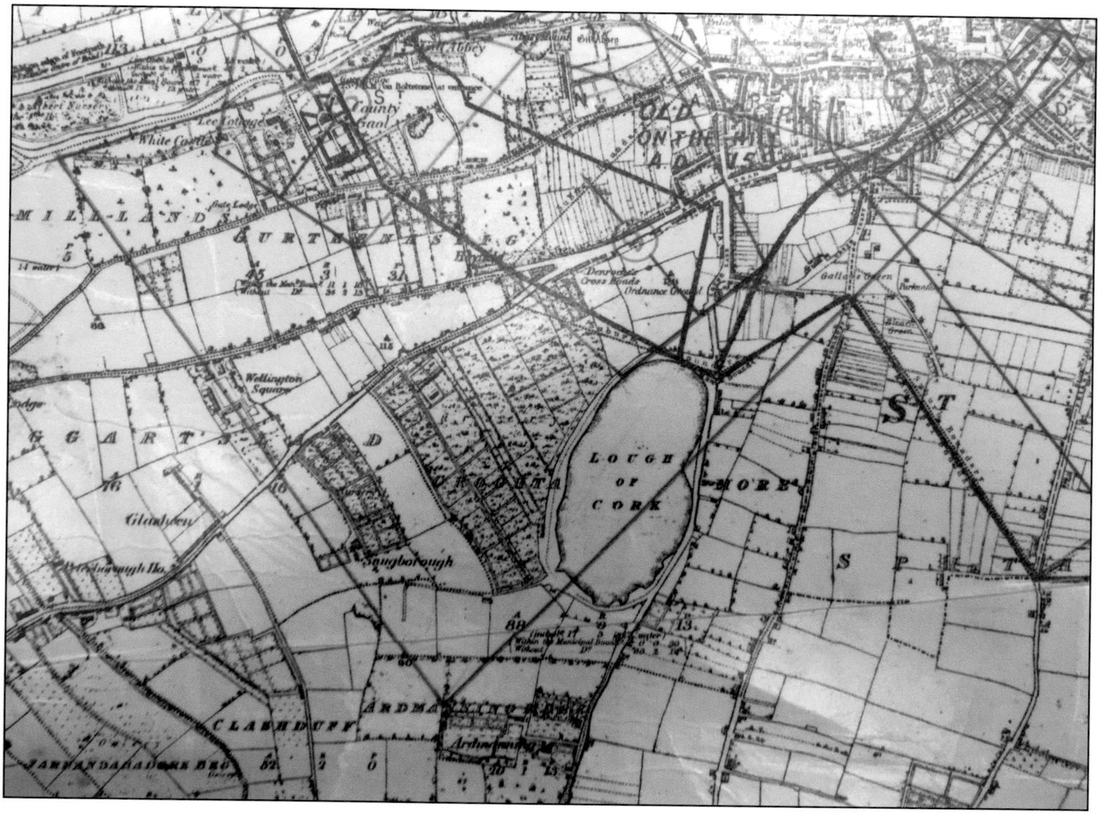

Map of The Lough, Cork, 1884. (Courtesy of Cork City Library)

and disappearing underground. Any excess of water is carried away by a gulley into the municipal sewer.

In 1659 the population in the immediate vicinity of The Lough consisted of four persons only, all Irish in descent. Some decades later, in 1690, during the Williamite Campaign in Ireland, a detachment of King William of Orange's army regrouped at The Lough prior to pressing the assault, which became known as the Siege of Cork.

In the early eighteenth century, the lands around the lake were deemed commonage lands and rented out by the Corporation of Cork. Indeed, from 21 October 1732 all 'black cattle' that stood in The Lough or on the ground about it in order to cool for slaughtering had to pay 1 penny for every head of such black cattle, a halfpenny for every pig or sheep. No freeman at large was liable to pay any of the duties as long the cattle belonged to such freeman.

During the eighteenth and nineteenth centuries, when it was frozen, ice skating took place on The Lough. Its banks hosted seasonal fairs. Some of the city's first suburban watchmen ran time trials around The Lough, and duels and even public punishment took place here. On the latter, in 1783, John Dwyer, Calvin Booth, John Fisher and James Ward, regimental foot soldiers who had been court-martialled for desertion, were taken to The Lough to suffer the consequences of their misbehaviour. Dwyer faced the firing squad, but the others got away with 500 lashes and transportation to Africa.

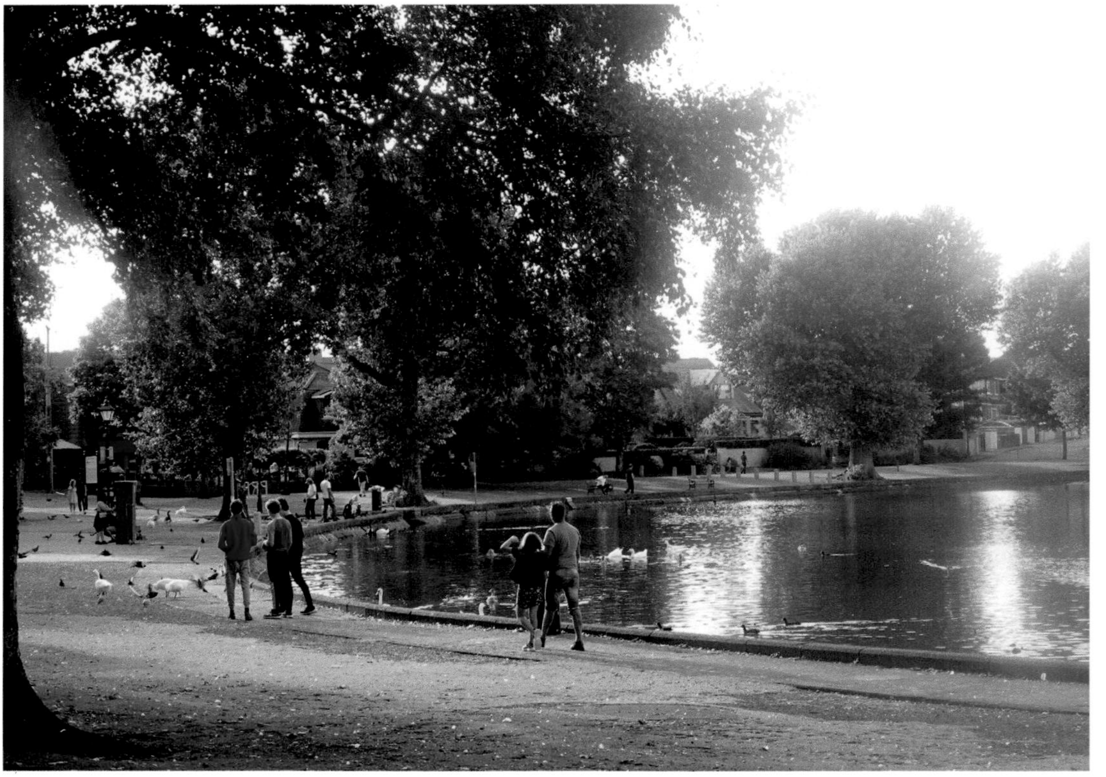

The Lough today.

2

The Legend of The Lough

During the nineteenth century Cork-born folklore collector Thomas Crofton Croker (1798–1854) collected the Legend of the Lough. This describes a scrupulous king who disallowed his citizens from obtaining water from his castle well. There followed a reckoning whereby a curse was played out: the castle was flooded out by the well and submerged by a lake, which is now The Lough.

Thomas had little school education but did read widely while working in the merchant trade. In 1813, he was apprenticed to a merchant in Cork. He managed to nurture the archaeological tastes he had acquired early on. He had considerable talent as an artist, and from the age of fourteen made several excursions in the south of Ireland, sketching and studying the character of the people.

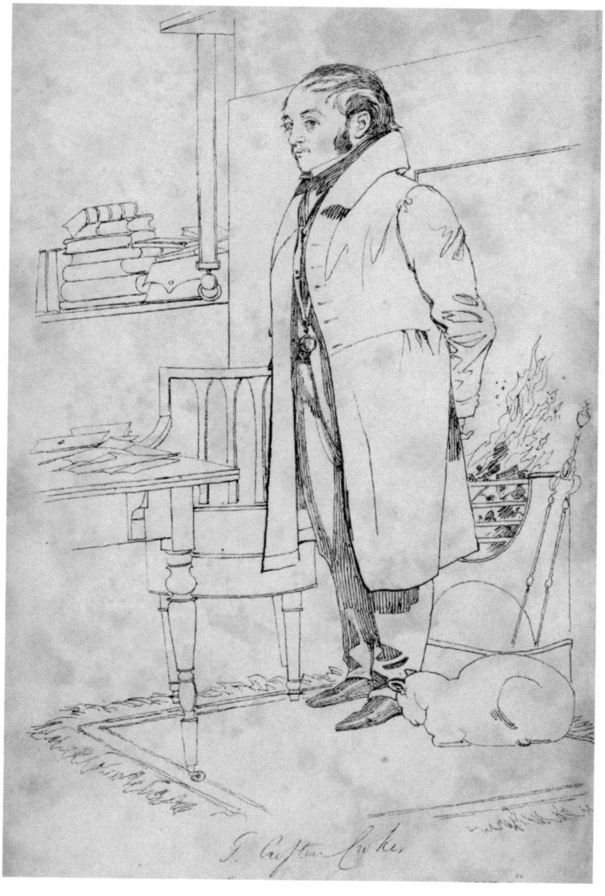

Thomas Crofton Croker by artist Daniel Maclise, 1829. (Courtesy of Cork City Library)

During his rambles in southern Ireland from 1812 to 1816, Thomas collected legends, folk songs and keens (dirges for the dead). He contributed sketches to local exhibitions and wrote occasionally for a local periodical. On his father's death in 1818 he went to London, where he obtained an appointment at the Admiralty through the influence of John W. Croker, a friend but no relative. He worked as a clerk in the Admiralty for thirty years.

In 1821 Thomas returned to southern Ireland and formed the plan of a tome published in 1824 called *Researches in the South of Ireland.* Thomas was twenty-six years of age on its publication. The success of his next work, *Fairy Legends and Traditions of the South of Ireland,* published anonymously in 1825, was so marked that he wrote a second series, illustrated by artist Daniel Maclise, which met with as favourable a reception. Both latter works were translated into German and French. They were translated into German by the Brothers Grimm.

Grimm's Fairy Tales, first published in Germany in 1812, were translated into English in 1823. The rise of Romanticism during the nineteenth century revived interest in traditional folk stories, which to the brothers represented a pure form of national literature and culture. They established a methodology for collecting and recording folk stories that became the basis for modern folklore studies.

Thomas Crofton Croker retired from government service in 1850 on a pension of £580 and died at No. 3 Gloucester Road, Old Brompton, London, on 8 August 1854, aged fifty-six. He was buried in London's Brompton Cemetery.

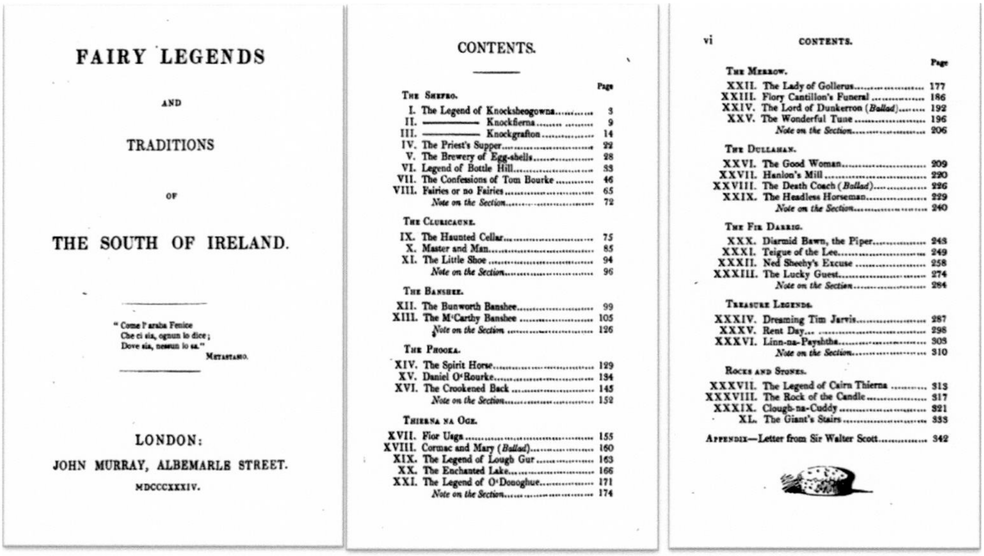

FAIRY LEGENDS

AND

TRADITIONS

OF

THE SOUTH OF IRELAND.

"Come l' araba Fenice
Che ci sia, ognun lo dice;
Dove sia, nessun lo sa."

METASTASIO.

LONDON:

JOHN MURRAY, ALBEMARLE STREET.

MDCCCXXXIV.

CONTENTS.

vi CONTENTS.

Front pages of *Fairy Legends and Traditions of the South of Ireland* by Thomas Crofton Croker. (Courtesy of Cork City Library)

3

For the People and By the People, St Finbarr's West Church

On Sunday 11 December 1881, a new Roman Catholic church overlooking The Lough was blessed by William Delaney, then Bishop of Cork, and named Church of the Immaculate Conception. This church was designed by George C. Ashlin and built by Barry MacMullen. It could seat 600 people.

Initially, the church was built as a chapel of ease to the parish church, St Finbarr's South at Dunbarr Street. The Lough church became known locally as 'St Finbarr's West'.

Nine years later, on 4 April 1890, Revd James Fleming announced to the congregation the creation of the new parish of St Finbarr's West and his appointment as parish priest.

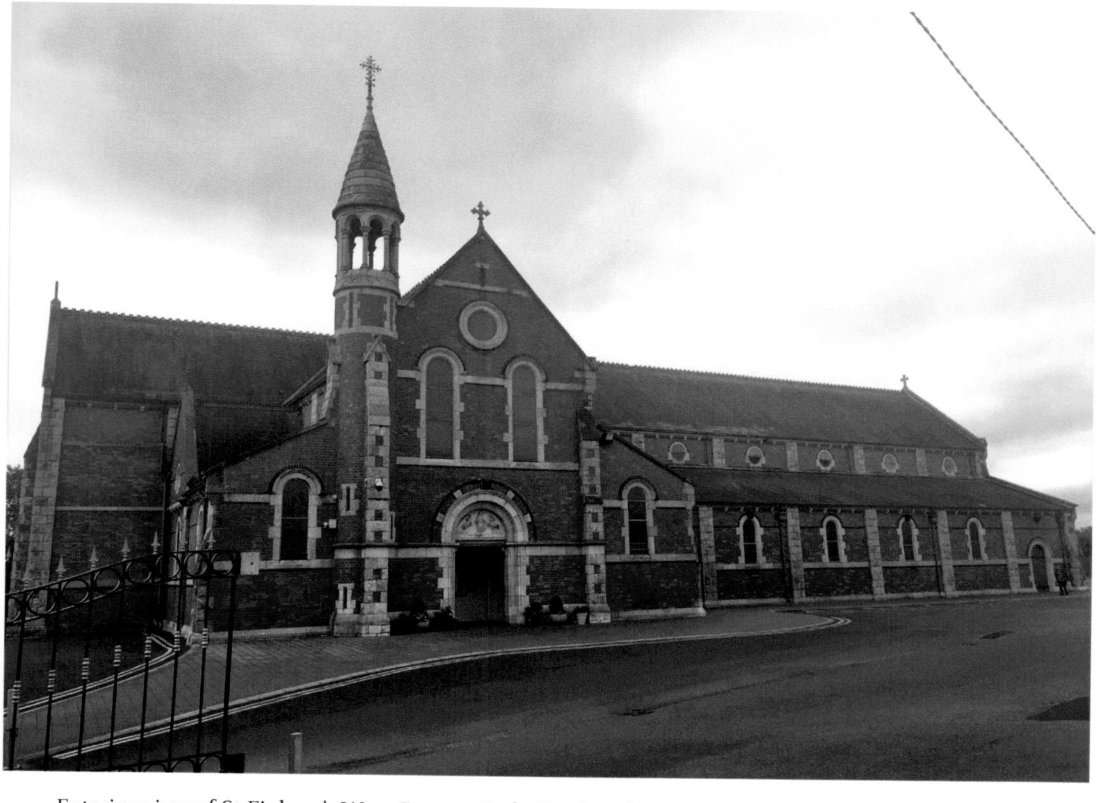

Exterior view of St Finbarr's West, Roman Catholic Church.

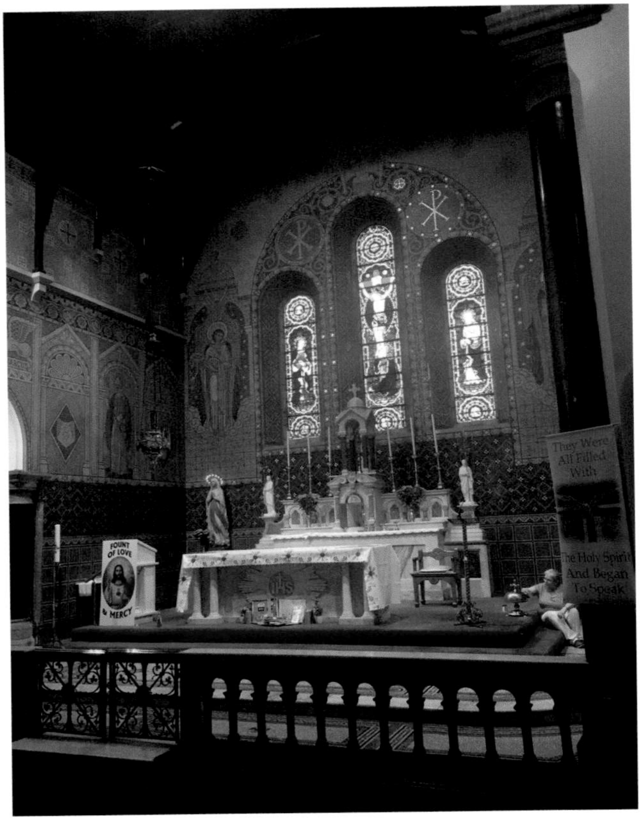

View of altar of St Finbarr's West, Roman Catholic Church.

By now the church's original accommodation was insufficient. Two transepts were built to accommodate another 150 people. A mortuary chapel was also added.

As time went on it became apparent that a much larger church was again needed, but the cost of building was prohibitive. In the late 1920s Canon Thomas Paris asked architect James McMullen to draw up plans for an addition to the existing structure. He converted the nave of the old church into transepts for the new one, and built a new 132-foot-long nave towards the west. The new extension incorporated side aisles and a west front. The crossing of the transept with the nave is an important feature of the Lough church. Four black marble clustered columns with limestone bases and caps surmounted by arches give good proportions to the setting of the sanctuary.

The main marble altar, which was originally purchased from the Dominican order for £80, is an excellent example of local workmanship. Castle island red marble plasters support a moulded cornice over the tabernacle; four columns of Aberdeen granite carry the canopy up; and the dorm and cross of white marble are supported by eight columns of Aberdeen marble.

On Sunday 3 March 1929, Bishop Daniel Cohalan solemnly blessed the renovated, enlarged and present-day church. The funding for it came from locals – a grand total of £21,000.

4

Gallows Green

Adjacent St Finbarr's West Church on the intersection of Gould Street and Green Street is the infamous site of Gallows Green. It was here that more malicious criminals, such as murderers and anti-Crown supporters, were hanged next to one of the city's largest southern-approach roads. Earliest records are from the mid-seventeenth century and the last number of executions were just before the Irish Great Famine. It was at that point that acts of hanging were moved to outside the entrances of the city's city and county gaols, respectively.

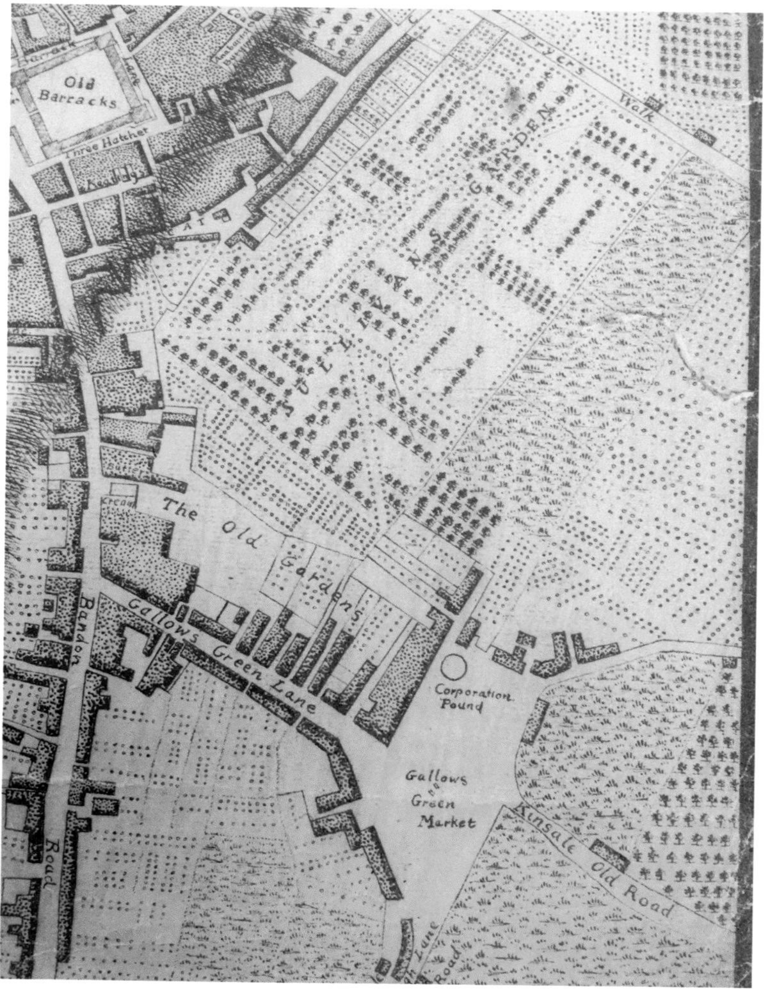

Map of Gallows Green from John Rocque's 'Map of Cork', 1773. (Courtesy of Cork City Library)

One of the earliest recorded executions took place at the gallows in 1644 when Lady Roche Viscountess Fermoy refused to renounce her religion. She was deemed one of the first high-profile Catholics to be hanged. In 1798, it is well recorded that Cork men involved in the United Irishmen were hanged en mass at Gallows Green.

Gallows Green was still a focal point of public gathering, especially in 1843 for Fr Mathew's temperance campaign and his public orations. The site though was subsumed into new housing developments in the later nineteenth century, with just the memory of the gallows surviving.

However, the memory of Gallows Green and the location where all the bodies were placed came to surface thirty years ago. In July 1990, human remains were uncovered in the back garden of a private residence in Greenmount, Cork City. The original ground level of the garden was almost 2 metres higher than the ground level of the house. It was while reducing the level of the garden that bones were discovered. At least fifteen individuals were recovered from the area. None of the skeletons were complete and many of the bones were broken. In one area all the long bones were stacked neatly together, with the skulls lying close by.

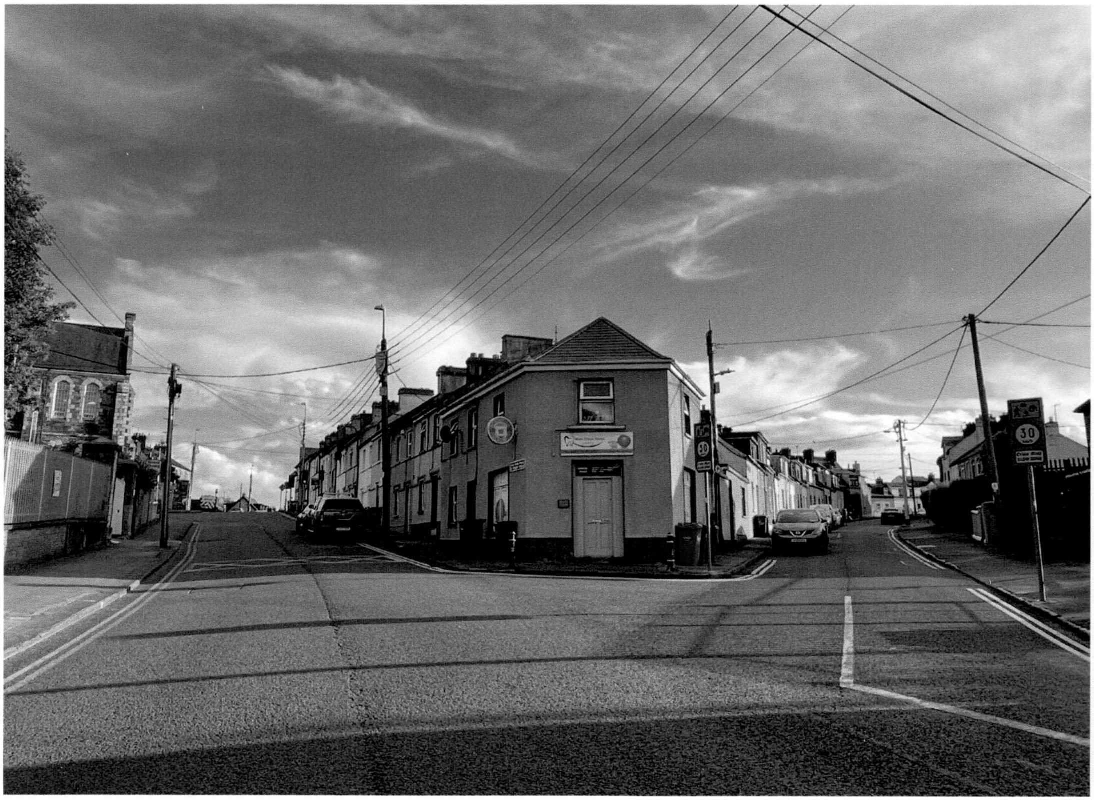

Present-day site of the Gallows Green intersection of Gould Street and Green Street.

5

Greenmount Industrial School

In recent years the stories and realities of Ireland's industrial schools have been well documented by the 'Commission to Inquire into Child Abuse', otherwise known as the Ryan Report (2009). Industrial and reformatory institutions were run by religious orders and funded by the public. In 1915, there were five reformatories and sixty-six industrial schools in Ireland. Eight of the latter were for boys under ten years old, who were then transferred to senior schools. From the Industrial Schools Act of 1868 to the eventual decline of industrial schools in 1969, over 105,000 children in Ireland were placed in this state care system.

Cork had two industrial schools 100 years ago: the Greenmount Industrial School (for boys) and St Finbarr's (for girls), which was based within the Good Shepherd Convent complex at Sunday's Well adjacent its Magdalen Asylum and Laundry. Information on St Finbarr's is difficult to source. There is a report of the Irish government's 'Inter-Departmental Committee to establish the facts of State involvement with the Magdalen Laundries (2013)'. It mentions St Finbarr's Industrial School, but there is nothing substantial. There is much work to be pursued on its history and the reality of attending there.

The Ryan Report outlines a detailed historical timeline of Greenmount Industrial School. It opened in 1871. By the turn of the twentieth century, it was certified to take

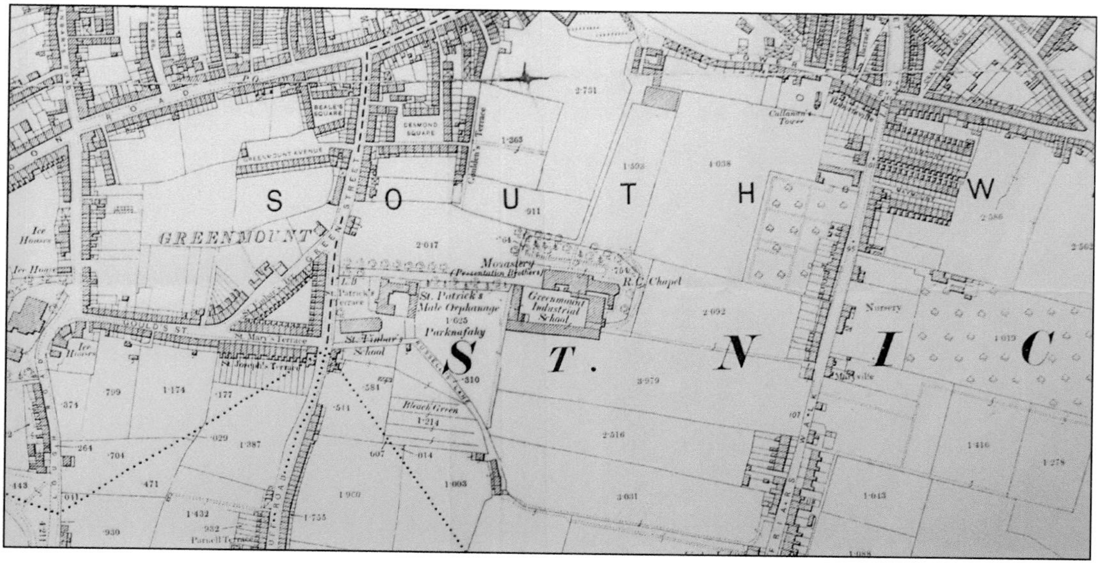

Map of Greenmount Industrial School, 1900.

in 200 boys and work was progressing on the grounds to include a farm. The goal was to provide the boys with training in farm work and at the same time provide food for the school along with an additional income from the sale of farm produce. The school was constructed on 8 acres, and the staff and boys in the school began cultivating the surrounding land. The Presentation Brothers continued to develop the farm. They purchased much of the surrounding land at the turn of the century; the adjacent farm comprised approximately 39 acres by the early twentieth century.

Greenmount Industrial School also had two further farms located at Lehenagh, on the outskirts of the city. It is recorded in the school annals that the management decided to sell these farms because of difficulties arising in the day-to-day management of them. The Department of Education records described the farm: 'The farm attached to this school has an area of 39 acres. It is used to supply milk and potatoes to the institution. Fifteen cows are kept and the feeding for these is grown on the farm.'

The school formally ceased operation on 31 March 1959. The school buildings no longer survive, the site now covered by the housing of Deerpark Road and Ros Barra.

6

That South American Link – Daniel Florence O'Leary

On the corner of Barrack Street and Green Street check out the plaque to Daniel Florence O'Leary. He was a military general and aide-de-camp under South American leader Simón Bolívar. Daniel was born *c.* 1802 in Nos 89/90 Barrack Street, Cork. His father was Jeremiah O'Leary, who was a butter merchant. Daniel emigrated to South America in 1817 to enlist in the fight for Venezuelan independence from the Spanish. In the early nineteenth century he climbed through the ranks of the army to become aide-de-camp to military leader Simón Bolívar during the South American Wars of Independence.

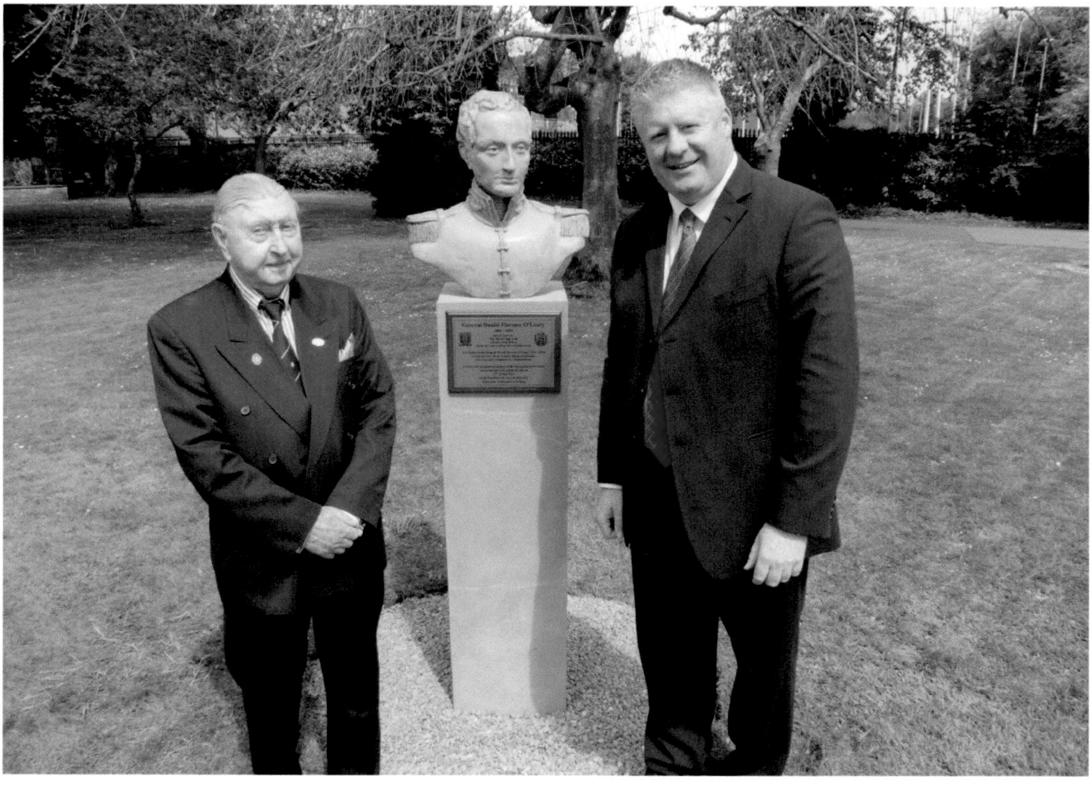

Unveiling the bust of Daniel Florence O'Leary with Michael O'Leary and Councillor Mick Finn at Fitzgerald's Park, 5 May 2010.

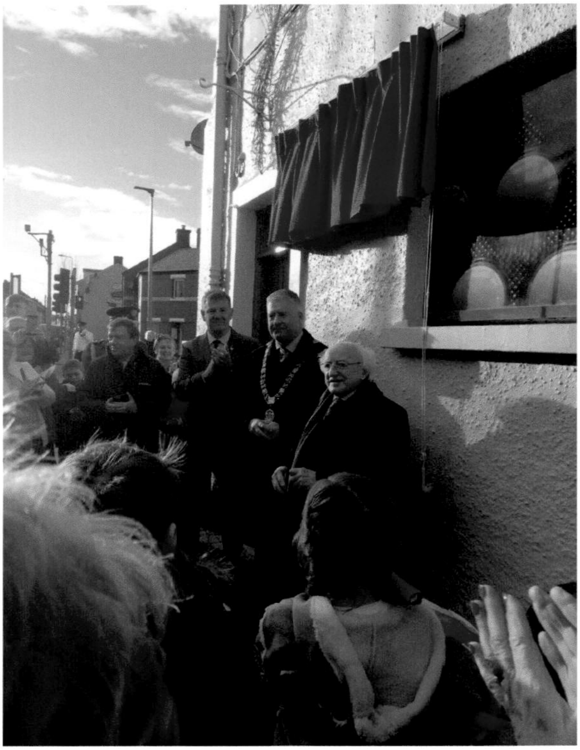

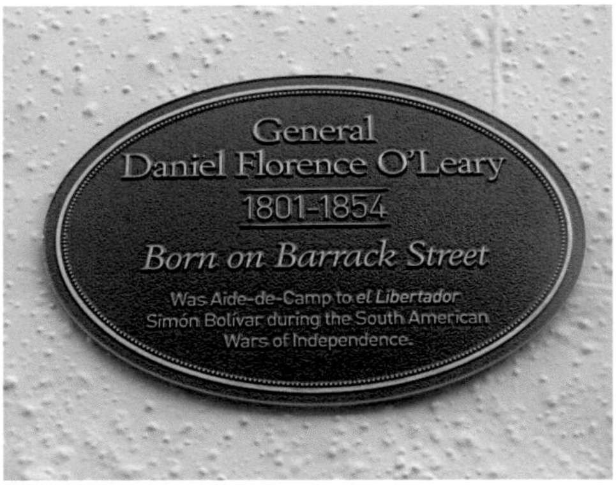

Above: Commemoration plaque to Daniel Florence O'Leary, Barrack Street.

Left: President of Ireland Michael D. Higgins with Lord Mayor of Cork Councillor Mick Finn, unveiling the Barrack Street commemoration plaque to Daniel Florence O'Leary, 2019. (Courtesy of Cork City Council)

Daniel is regarded as a great diplomat, military leader and hero in northern South America, and in Venezuela especially. His tomb is in the National Pantheon of Venezuela in Caracas and is guarded by a twenty-four-hour guard.

After Bolívar's death, O'Leary disobeyed orders to burn the general's personal papers. He spent much of the rest of his life organising those papers, along with writing his very extensive memories (spanning thirty-four volumes) of his time fighting in the wars of revolution with Bolívar. Daniel died in 1854 and his memory is recalled in a city centre plaza in Caracas.

In 2010 by the Venezuelan ambassador to Ireland, Dr Samuel Moncada, presented a bust and plaque honouring O'Leary. They were a gift by the Venezuelan government to the people of Cork and unveiled in Fitzgerald's Park. It was a relative of Daniel Florence, the late historian Michael O'Leary, who was a relative of the general and who worked so hard to ensure he would be remembered in his native city.

A plaque to Daniel Florence O'Leary on Barrack Street was unveiled by President Michael D. Higgins in February 2019 with the then Lord Mayor of Cork, Cllr Mick Finn.

7

In Context, Barrack Street

Barrack Street is the oldest of the city's approach roads into its centre. Excavation work in 2000 by Sheila Lane Archaeologists at the Flying Enterprise Bar by South Gate Bridge revealed pieces of a late Viking timber track. It was dated to AD 1085.

In October 2021, archaeological investigations at, and adjoining, the site of the former Nancy Spain's public house, Barrack Street, Cork, have revealed a previously unknown exceptionally large defensive cut feature (ditch), which through radiocarbon dating has been dated to the period between the early eleventh and mid-twelfth centuries, a time when the city was being developed by the Hiberno-Scandinavians – descendants of the Vikings who had intermixed with native Irish people.

Mr David Murphy, the archaeologist who excavated the site in connection with city council archaeologist Ciara Brett, stated the following on the impressive finds:

> The presence of this defensive ditch feature, some 300 metres upslope and to the southwest of the accepted area of settlement, may suggest that the settlement was more extensive than previously thought. Alternatively, and perhaps more likely, is that a defensive ditch feature, which enclosed the lower lying settlement, was dug into the higher ridgeline above the riverside settlement. The ability to defend the higher ground above the settlement

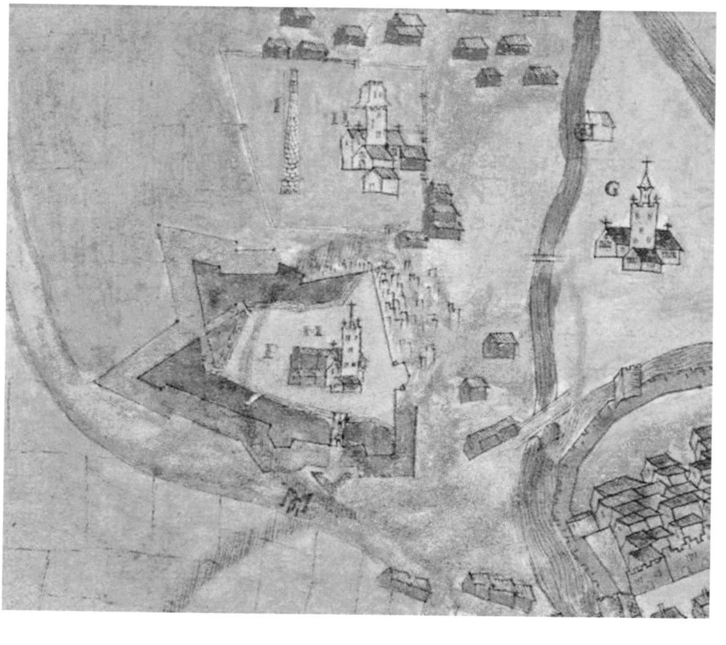

Elizabeth Fort from *A Description of the Cittie of Cork Plan of Cork, circa* 1602. (Courtesy of Cork City Library)

> would dispossess any potential attackers of a significant strategic advantage. If this theory is correct, the ditch would most likely extend in an elongated curved manner and roughly follow the alignment of Vicar Street and Tower Street for a portion of its route.

It is only in George Carew's colourful Plan of Cork (*c.* 1601) where one gets a sketch of Barrack Street. In this plan the emphasis is less on the height of the town walls and more on the wide roads leading into the settlement. It is the showcasing of Elizabeth Fort (with the Holy Rood Church within) which is perhaps why this map might have been created. Such a fort was also responsible for giving the name Barrack Street to the adjacent routeway.

The 2021 archaeological investigations at, and adjoining, the site of the former Nancy Spain's pub revealed the burials of six individuals. The skeletal remains of four of these individuals were uncovered within a mass burial pit and had evidently met a violent end. Ms Niamh Daly, the osteo-archaeologist, in her report outlined that small fragments of bone taken from two of the skeletons to facilitate radiocarbon dating have returned dates from the period between AD 1447 and 1636.

Fast forward to the Siege of Cork (1690) and the area of Barrack Street was involved in a stand-off between James II supporters and Williamite forces. The James II supporters retreated into the town, but first set fire to the southern suburbs – the area now occupied by Douglas Street, Cove Street and Barrack Street. The main upshot was the almost complete rebuilding of the street. There are several historic plaques on the present-day street, which reflect the reconstruction of buildings in the early eighteenth century, supplemented by additions in the nineteenth century.

Guy's Directory of Cork for 1922 has two pages dedicated to Barrack Street. It records that out of 148 properties there were twenty-five vintners, thirty-six shopkeepers and eight provision dealers as well as a large potato and fish market. Bootmakers, builders, chemists, confectioners, dairy stores, drapers, dress makers, dyers, flour stores, fruiterers, hairdressers, lodging houses, laundry receiving houses, milliners, pawnbrokers, tailors and victuallers are all recorded.

The glory of Barrack Street may have faded in recent years, with many of the trades from a century ago long gone, but urban renewal schemes are breathing new life into Cork's historic street.

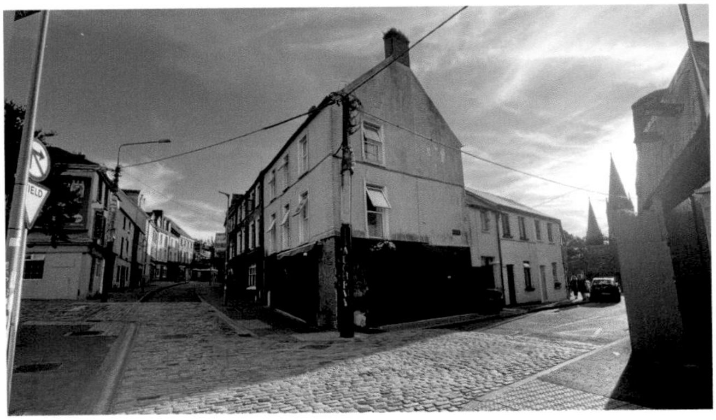

Barrack Street.

8

The Place of Elizabeth Fort

Much has been written on Elizabeth Fort, from its construction in 1601 to protect the walled town, to it becoming a tourism centre in recent years. The mini-information centre within the fort speaks about it only being attacked once in its 400-year history.

In September 1690, the Siege of Cork tested the strength of the fort immensely. In short, James II's supporters possessed Elizabeth Fort and the Williamite forces had to dominate at least two tall adjacent buildings – Red Abbey and St Fin Barre's Cathedral – to rain down shots on the Irish in the area in order to attain surrender. It is unfortunate that much of the documentation describing the layout and rebuilding of the fort from the early eighteenth century to the present day has been lost. All that is known is that the encompassing star-shaped bastion remained unchanged.

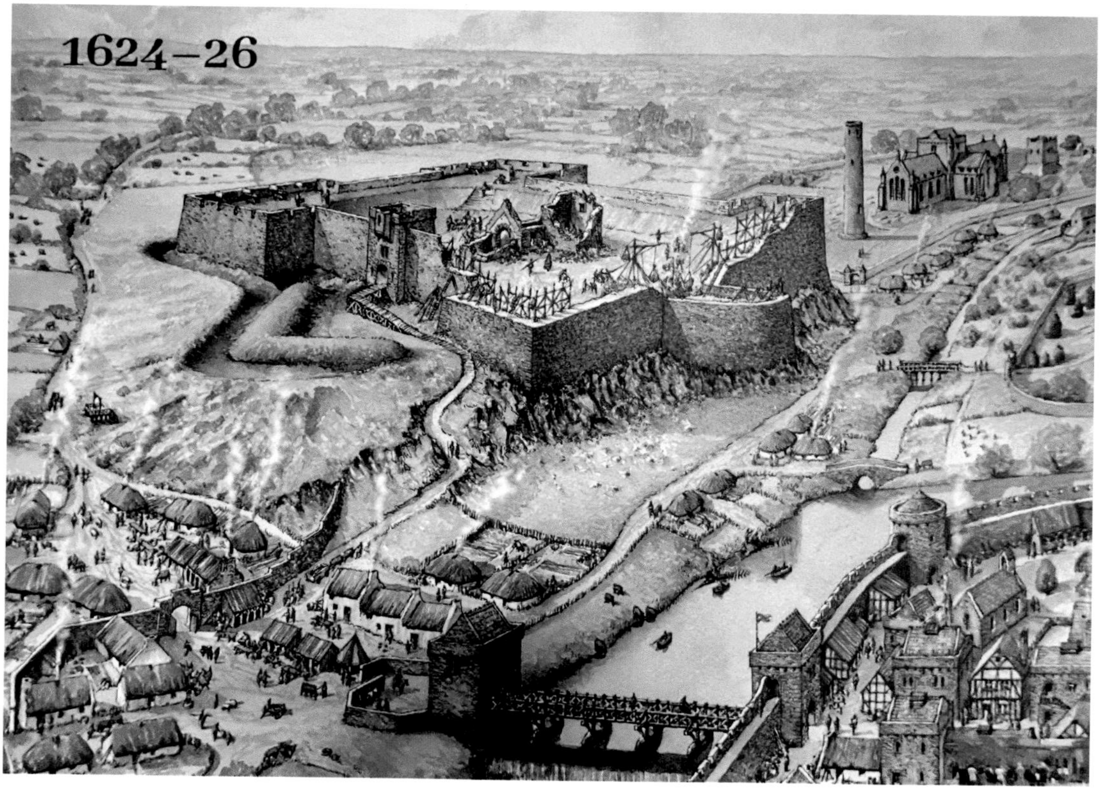

Reconstruction of life at Elizabeth Fort and surrounds, *c*. 1624. (Illustration by Philip Armstrong and commissioned by Cork City Council; courtesy of Cork City Council)

It is known that in 1719 Elizabeth Fort became a British military barracks and catered for 700 men. An additional square barracks known as Cat Barracks (established in 1698) existed nearby. Historic maps of Cork from the late seventeenth century show that Cat Barracks was a type of exterior moat defence to Elizabeth Fort.

In 1806, due to the construction of the 'New Barracks' to the north-east of the city (now Collin's Barracks), the barracks within Elizabeth fort were altered to that of a Female Convict Prison.

In the late nineteenth century, the fort was used as a station for the Cork City Artillery Militia. In 1920–21, it was occupied by the Royal Irish Constabulary and handed over to the Provisional Government of Ireland. A year later, in 1922, it is known that the existing interior buildings of the fort were burned down by anti-treaty forces. The walls and bastions of the fort were undamaged. A few years later a Garda Station was set up in the interior of the fort, which today is still in operation.

Elizabeth Fort remains one of Cork's most historic gems and its on-site heritage centre remains one of the ever-evolving heritage projects of Cork City Council.

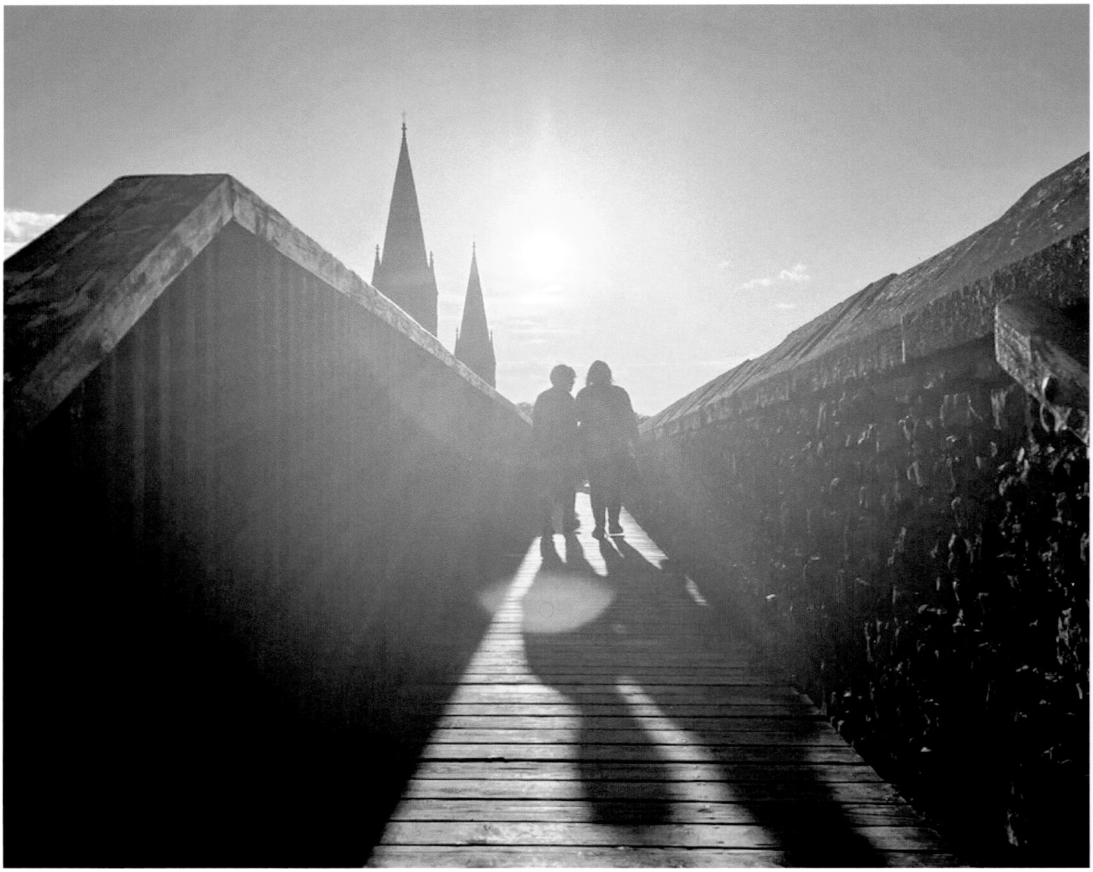

An autumn sunset at Elizabeth Fort.

9

An Arch of Somewhere – From Leper Colony to Hospital

The blocked-up archway on Stephen Street is one of very few nods to the Barrack Street area before being built up with housing. The arch approximately marks the ground of the medieval St Stephen's Church, whose physical presence is long gone.

The publication *Burial Grounds of Cork* (2011) by Hillary Kelleher and Fintan McCarthy, and edited by Ciara Brett, highlights at least six churches with burial grounds built in the late twelfth century onwards in the southern suburbs around what is now the Barrack Street and its surrounds. These included St Mary del Nard Church (now marked by Elizabeth Fort), St Brigid's Church (now St James Square), St John's the Evangelist, Benedictine Church (formerly the White Street car park area), St John the Baptist Church (now the Parkowen site), St Michael's Church (adjacent the present-day Elizabeth Fort) and St Stephen's Church (formerly adjacent Stephen Street). Some of the graveyards of these

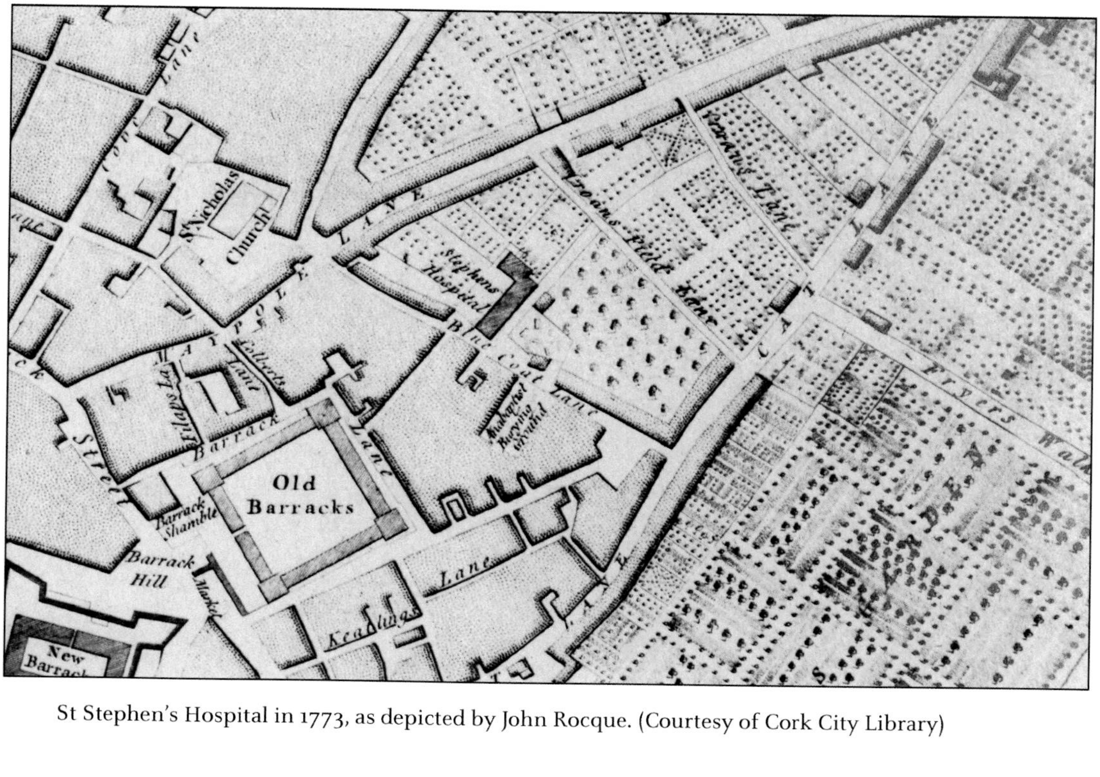

St Stephen's Hospital in 1773, as depicted by John Rocque. (Courtesy of Cork City Library)

latter churches would have still served the late seventeenth- and early eighteenth-century population.

Connected to St Stephen's Church or Priory was a leper house, erected in 1250, of which Edward Henry was 'Custas' or keeper in 1295. The house remained a hospital for many centuries until it was suppressed and closed during the Reformation. Much of the lands eventually came into the possession of William Worth, Recorder of Cork, who, by a deed penned in 1699, transferred them to the Corporation.

In the first decade of the eighteenth century the Corporation of Cork wished to erect a house, to be called St Stephen's Hospital, for many poor boys of the Protestant religion. The nomination process was in the hands of the mayor and Corporation members. In essence, the hospital house was a school, which became known as Blue Coat School (after part of the boy's uniform). The boys were to be eight years of age on admission and be apprenticed at fourteen years of age.

The trades that former boys of the school were apprenticed to make interesting reading. Historic registers detail apprenticeships such as block and pump makers, cordwainers, weavers, wool combers and dyers, brush makers, stay makers, whip makers, nailors, pewterers, hatters, curriers, glass cutters, copperplate printers and writing clerks.

When the municipal Reform Act was passed in 1840, the mayor and council were abolished as governors of the hospital and the school was funded by Protestant merchants in the city. During 1916 the closing of the school was sanctioned. Dwelling houses have since been built on the site, and the entrance archway is the only remaining feature.

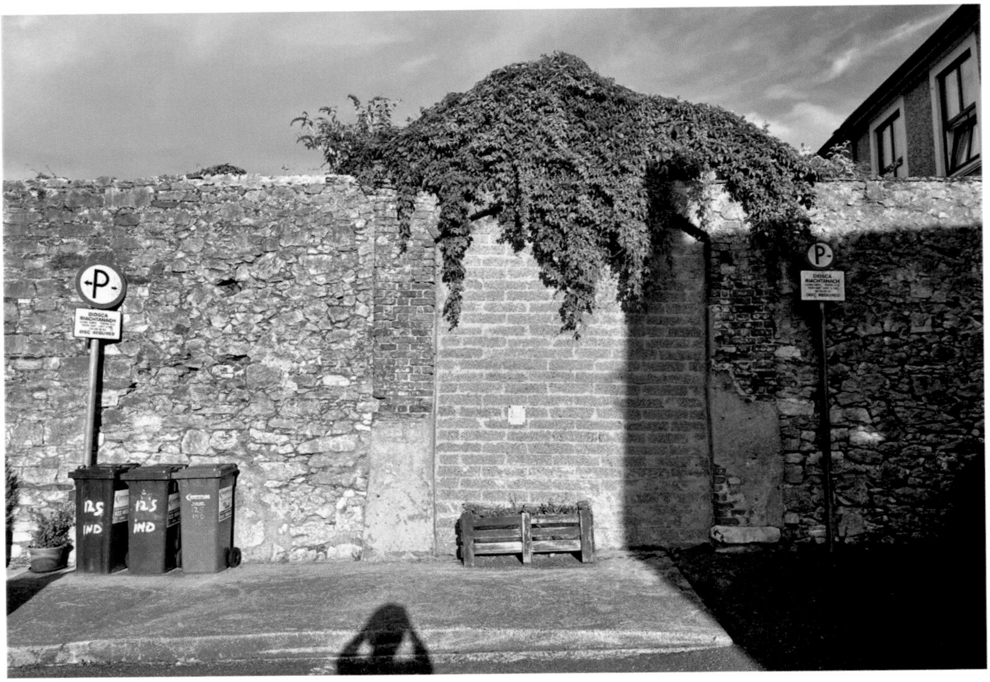

Blocked entrance to Blue Coat School.

The John Sisk Housing Projects

On 21 October 1921, there was deep regret felt by the citizens of Cork. John Sisk, builder, died at his residence at No. 1 Cove Street at the age of eighty-four. The deceased gentleman was well known not only in Cork but throughout Munster. He was prominently identified with the building trade for more than half a century. In later years he had the assistance of his sons Nicholas, Richard and John. The firm erected many of the finest churches in Munster, and perhaps their largest contract was the building of the head offices of the Munster and Leinster Bank on the South Mall in 1912.

According to the 1911 census, John Sisk was born in County Cork on 30 September 1837. At the age of eleven he followed in the footsteps of his father Patrick and was apprenticed to a Quaker plasterer named Robert Martin.

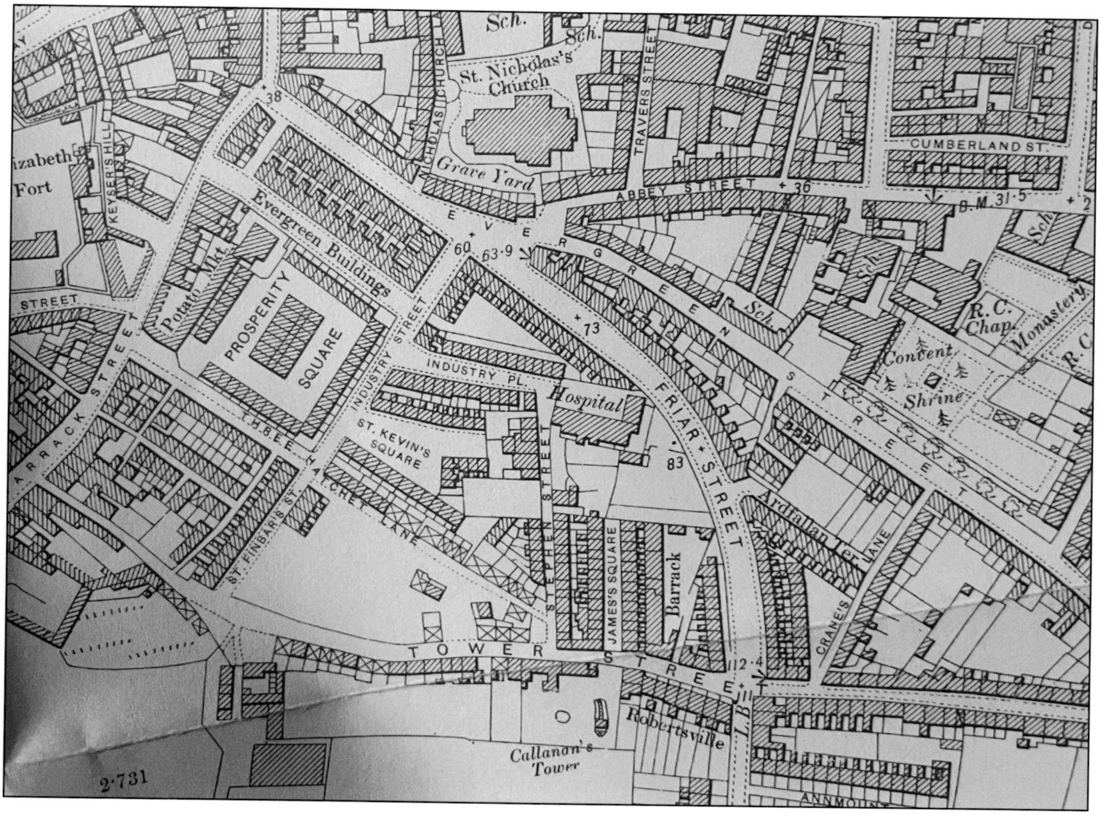

Map of Sisk housing and the Cork Improved Dwelling Company, just off Barrack Street, 1900. (Courtesy of Cork City Library)

Shortly before his first marriage in 1859, John set up in business as a builder in Cork. He progressed to become one of the leading contractors in the south of Ireland and became connected with several major architects working in Ireland in the late nineteenth and early twentieth centuries. Much of his work was ecclesiastical. As an offshoot of his church-building interests, he became involved in Roman Catholic charitable work. As a lifelong teetotaller, he became vice-president of the Cork Catholic Young Men's Society for many years.

John was married twice: first in 1859, to Catherine (née Burke), then in 1890/91 to Ellen. Of his six sons from his first marriage, four were involved in the building trades.

In the area of Barrack Street it is John's series of red-bricked housing developments that stands out, such on St Kevin's Square, St Finbarr's Street, St Brigid Street and on St Nessan Street. Such developments were first proposed in May 1892 when John Sisk came before the Corporation of Cork and submitted plans for 150 houses for the working classes. He wished to erect them on land that was being used as a dump for rubbish. Nearby were the successful Cork Improved Dwellings Company housing projects from the 1880s – i.e. Evergreen Buildings and Prosperity Square.

John Sisk proposed to spend the sum of £20,000, and when built the houses would bring in a revenue and rates of about £400 to the Corporation of Cork. The plans were approved by the Corporation and sent to the Board of Works. However, due to prolonged legal issues, construction did not take place for over ten years – in the first decade of the twentieth century.

Today John Sisk & Son Ltd is Ireland's largest and oldest construction company and one of Europe's top construction companies.

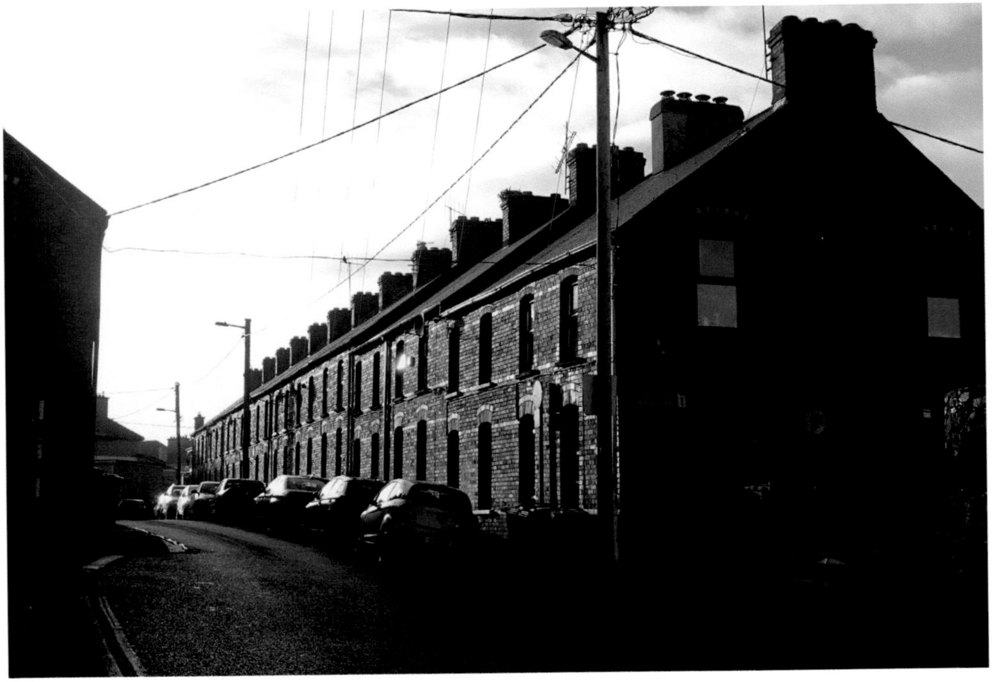

St Finbarr's Street, off Barrack Street.

11

Cove Street and St Nicholas Church

The advent of Norwegian Vikings in AD 820 and Danish Vikings *c.* AD 914 marked the early origins of Cork as a port. These new invaders started off by raiding the monastery on the hillside, but soon turned their attention to neighbouring powerful and wealthier political kingdoms in Munster. One such local kingdom was that of Fir Maige in southern Munster.

Historians of Cork through the centuries have proposed that one that Danish area of settlement was located south of the site of Fin Barre's monastery on the southern hillside, extending from what is now Frenches Quay/the Barrack Street area through Cove Street to the area of Georges Quay.

Cove Street itself is reputedly named after a cove for ships. It is said that at one time the River Lee occupied an area immediately north of the street, an area that was subsequently reclaimed by the seventeenth century. Maps from the early 1700s show that George's Quay was only constructed sometime between 1750 and 1773.

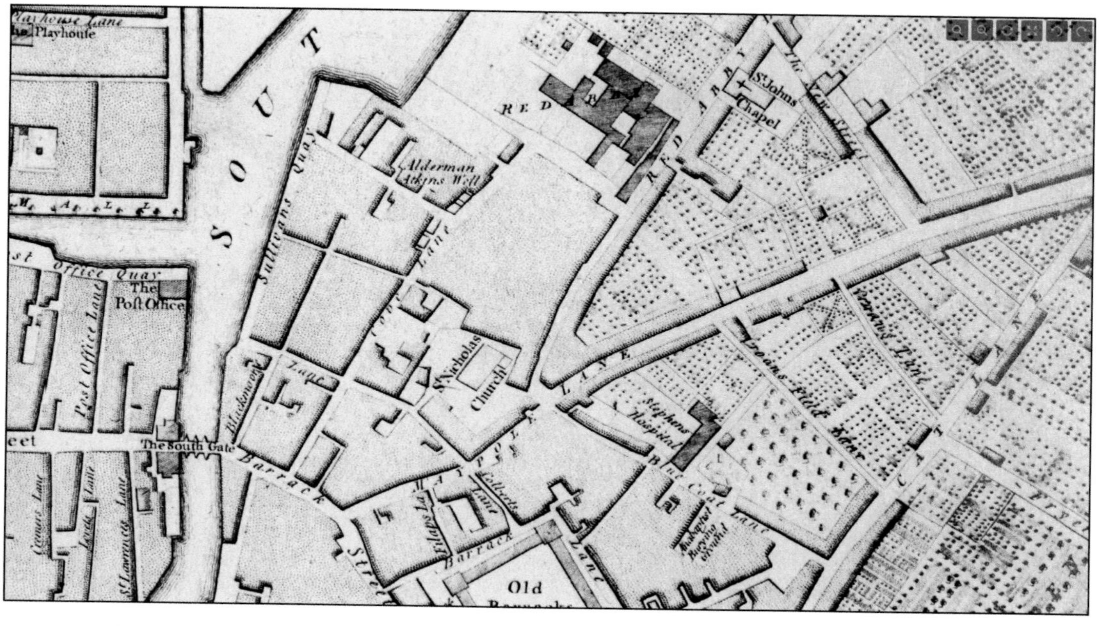

St Nicholas Church and the surrounding area, 1773. (Courtesy of Cork City Library)

Soaring over Cove Street is St Nicholas Church, which was erected initially in honour of the Anglo-Norman victory over the Danish settlers in Cork in 1174. The Anglo-Norman church of St Nicholas was registered by its clergy in 1270 and granted by the Bishop of Cork to St Thomas' Abbey, Dublin. The cult of St Nicholas was quite popular in medieval times, especially among seafarers as he was their patron saint.

Nearly 400 years later this church still stood. However, severe damage was caused to St Nicholas Church during the Siege of Cork in 1690. It was only in 1720 when funds were allocated by the Protestant Bishop of Cork, Peter Browne, that a new St Nicholas Church was built. Indeed, the finance for its construction came from the taxing of coal that was imported into Cork for domestic purposes.

Construction work on the new church began in 1720. In mid-June 1721, the Town Chamberlain paid £100 out of the coffers of the Corporation to Mr Archdeacon Ayers, the head builder of the church venture. Misfortune occurred again on 20 June 1726 when the eastern end of St Nicholas Church was greatly damaged by thunder and lightning. Repairs were duly initiated.

In 1850, a significant mid-nineteenth-century Gothic Revival Church replaced large parts of the earlier church on the same site. It was designed by Cork-born architect Joseph Welland, with the steeple by Atkins and transept windows by Hemmings.

In 1999 the church was de-consecrated and internal fittings and fixtures stripped out. Planning permission was granted to convert St Nicholas's Church, Cove Street, Cork, to office use. Sheila Lane, archaeologist, dug sixteen roughly square trenches, which were manually excavated for the construction of pads to support concrete columns in the church. Each trench was excavated to 0.65–0.9 metres below ground level. Four of the trenches encroached on east–west inhumations that pre-dated the existing church building and were probably connected with the graveyard of the eighteenth-century or the medieval church.

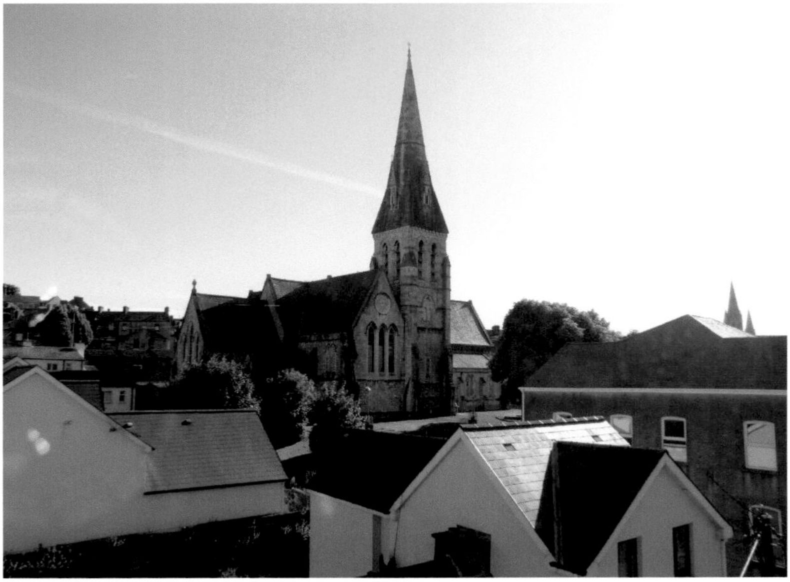

St Nicholas Church today.

12

Sullivan's Quay and the Christian Brothers

There were several free public schools in nineteenth-century Cork for the poorer members of Cork City. The most notable was operated by the Christian Brothers and known as the North Monastery, which was opened in 1811 with branch establishments at Blarney Street (northside) and Sullivan's Quay (southside). Together, over 2,000 boys of poor backgrounds received an excellent education.

Sullivan's Quay School was opened as the Christian Brothers' second school in the city in 1828. Dean Jeremiah Collins, parish priest of St Finbarr's South, followed the work of the North Monastery school closely and was impressed by its educational principles. Dean Collins asked the brothers to establish a school in the South Parish. A site was selected on Sullivan's Quay and while building work was being pursued classes started and took

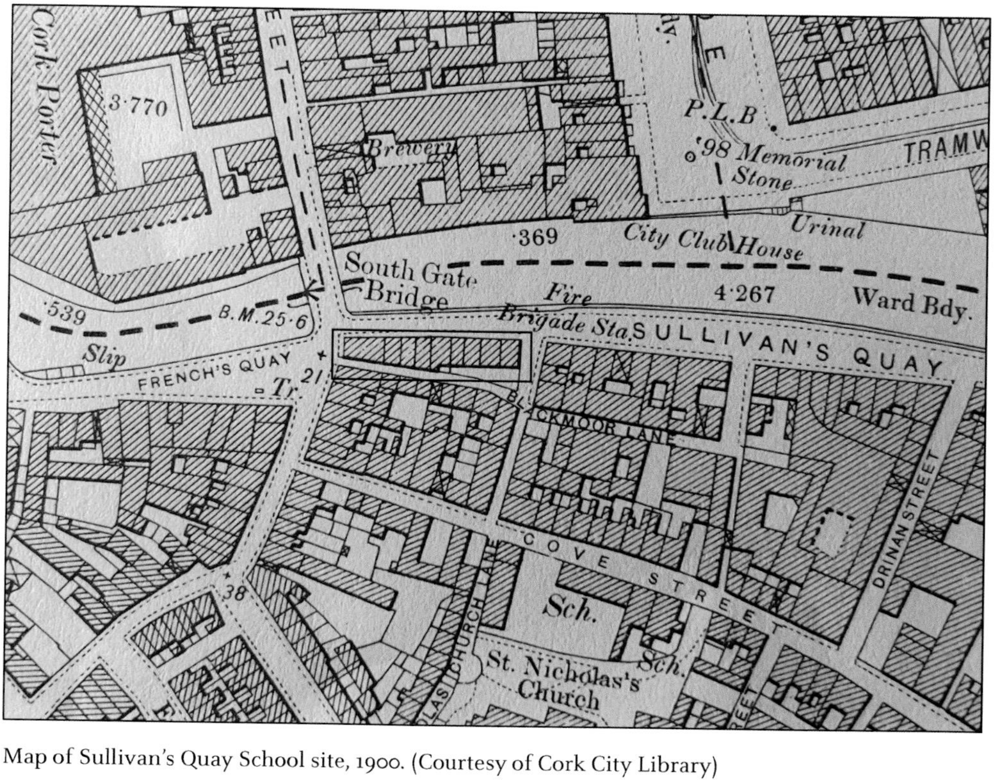

Map of Sullivan's Quay School site, 1900. (Courtesy of Cork City Library)

place in an old store loft on Cove Street. In 1828, the new school was opened comprising a two-floor building by the banks of the River Lee.

Fast forward to the turn of the twentieth century and the upper floor of the building had already been converted from its original two classrooms into three. This was deemed too small for the needs for the growing school population and an expansion project was decided upon. Tenants still occupied the ground floor and asking them to leave was not an easy request – some needed much persuasion to surrender their leases. The substantial rent of £53.60 per annum was also being given up on by the Brothers.

Renovations commenced before the summer of 1905 and were completed that winter, formally reopening on 27 October by Bishop O'Callaghan. The reconstruction of the school was to cost in the region of £2,200. In a detailed description, the *Cork Examiner* outlines that from the ground to the roof was reconstructed to include six classrooms, a suitable playground and improved toilets. A third floor was also added to help give height to the second floor. Designed by Samuel F. Hynes, work was completed by E&P Flynn, builders on Watercourse Road.

Approximately twenty-five years later, work began on a new and a larger school building on Cove Street to support the service on the quayside. On 13 September 1934, 400 boys were enrolled in the new school, which was named Saint Nessan.

Originally, the pupils who completed their primary education in the school had to go to the North Monastery to continue their secondary schooling. However, in 1949 the first leaving certificate exams took place in Sullivan's Quay. Years later the brothers acquired a property just off Friar's Walk in Deerpark. A new secondary school, Coláiste Iognaid Rís, was opened there in 1968.

Sullivan's Quay and Deerpark flourished for decades but unfortunately fell victim to population decline in the inner city. There was a strong exodus to the city, expanding the suburbs. In 1970, Sullivan Quay had 500 pupils and by the year of its closure just thirteen pupils remained in two classes in the quay. In 2006, both Sullivan's Quay and the other large centre of educational centre of South Presentation School closed. Sullivan's Quay is currently the property of the Flying Enterprise Bar and Courtyard with former classrooms being rented out for cultural and rehearsal purposes.

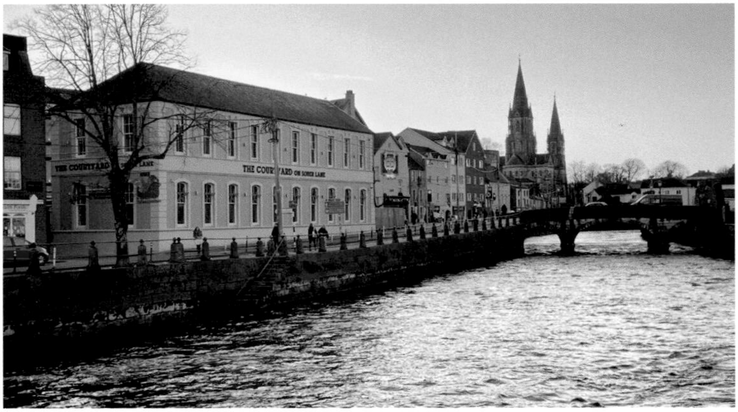

Former Sullivan's School site.

13

A War of Independence Ambush Site

As the Irish War of Independence intensified, the tit-for-tat violence continued in late September and into October 1920. Engineer Officer of the 2nd Battalion, Cork No. 1 Brigade, Michael O'Donoghue in his witness statement (WS1741) in the Bureau of Military History records he was twenty years of age running the intelligence, engineering and the signals and communications services. A Special Services unit was also organised and trained in Cork City. A few of the latter group were trained in machine gun use and assembling. These skills were put to full use during the autumn of 1920.

On the night of 7 October 1920, Michael recalls a further ambush scenario on Barrack Street. He happened to be in the shop owned by sisters Nora and Sheila Wallace in Cork's St Augustine Street. This shop was used as a clearing house for IRA dispatches and was a regular meeting place for IRA men generally. The Wallace sisters were active Cumann na mBan figures and were well respected in their collaboration with the brigade officers.

On the night in question, while in Wallace's with Seán Hegarty, Brigade Officer in Charge, an IRA member, came into the shop. He was a civilian employee in the military barracks, Cork, where he worked as a clerk in the British Military Intelligence office. On many occasions he had passed on information of great value. He told those present that a lorry of armed soldiers would be leaving Cork barracks the following day around 9 a.m. and would proceed across the city to Elizabeth Fort, off Barrack Street. Michael Murphy discussed the possibility of attacking the lorry with Seán Hegarty and it was agreed that Michael himself should undertake the job on the following morning, 8 October 1920. That night, after curfew, Michael contacted about twenty men from his battalion area and told them to be at the Thomas Ashe Hall, Father Mathew Quay, the following day around 8 a.m. They were to come armed with revolvers and grenades.

On the morning of 8 October Michael met the men in the hall as arranged and explained his proposed attack strategy on the military lorry. It was his intention to attack the military lorry himself along with Tadhg Sullivan, one of his company captains. They were to engage them with grenades and revolvers. The remainder of the party were then dispersed to positions covering the British military garrison at Elizabeth Fort and the police barracks at Tuckey Street and Union Quay. All of these posts were within a couple of hundred yards radius of the point in Barrack Street, where the proposed attack was to take place.

Michael and Tadhg took up position at a corner on the junction of Barrack Street and Cove Street where there was a steep incline. They knew the lorry would have to slow down to get in gear when it reached that point. At about 8.45 a.m. the lorry came into view. As expected, the lorry slowed down, and Michael saw that it contained three soldiers in the driver's cab and eight–ten inside in the open lorry section. He threw the first grenade, which hopped off the side of the lorry and exploded, wounding Tadhg and himself but

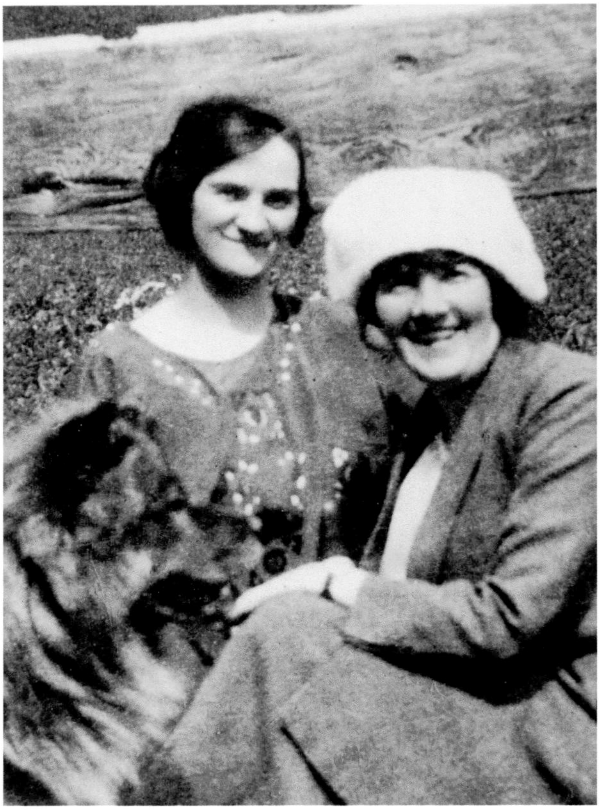

Nora and Sheila Wallace. (Courtesy of Cork Public Museum)

not seriously. Tadgh and Michael then hurled grenades into the cab, killing one of the private officers. The third grenade got into the back of the lorry, causing casualties among the soldiers there.

The lorry continued on up the hill and was met by a volley from revolver men stationed further up the road. Those soldiers who were not wounded now jumped out of the lorry and took refuge in nearby houses. The ambush lasted about fifteen minutes, then Michael ordered the lads to break off the attack due to a lack of ammunition and they scampered.

Reprisals by the Black and Tans for the Barrack Street Ambush on Friday 8 October and for the connected death of Private John Gordon Squibbs were quick. The stakes were heightened again when that Friday night City Hall (old) was targeted by the Tans for an arson attack. Even though it was not fully successful, much damage was caused. The attack commenced about 3.45 a.m., when a volley of shots was fired evidently from rifles at the building. The witness to the attack was the building's night watchman who described to the *Cork Examiner* how the events unfolded.

The fire brigade, under Captain Alfred Hutson, were not slow to arrive. Hoses were speedily laid, and water was soon poured into the Public Health and Waterworks offices. At first the flames spread with alarming rapidity, and at one time it looked as if that

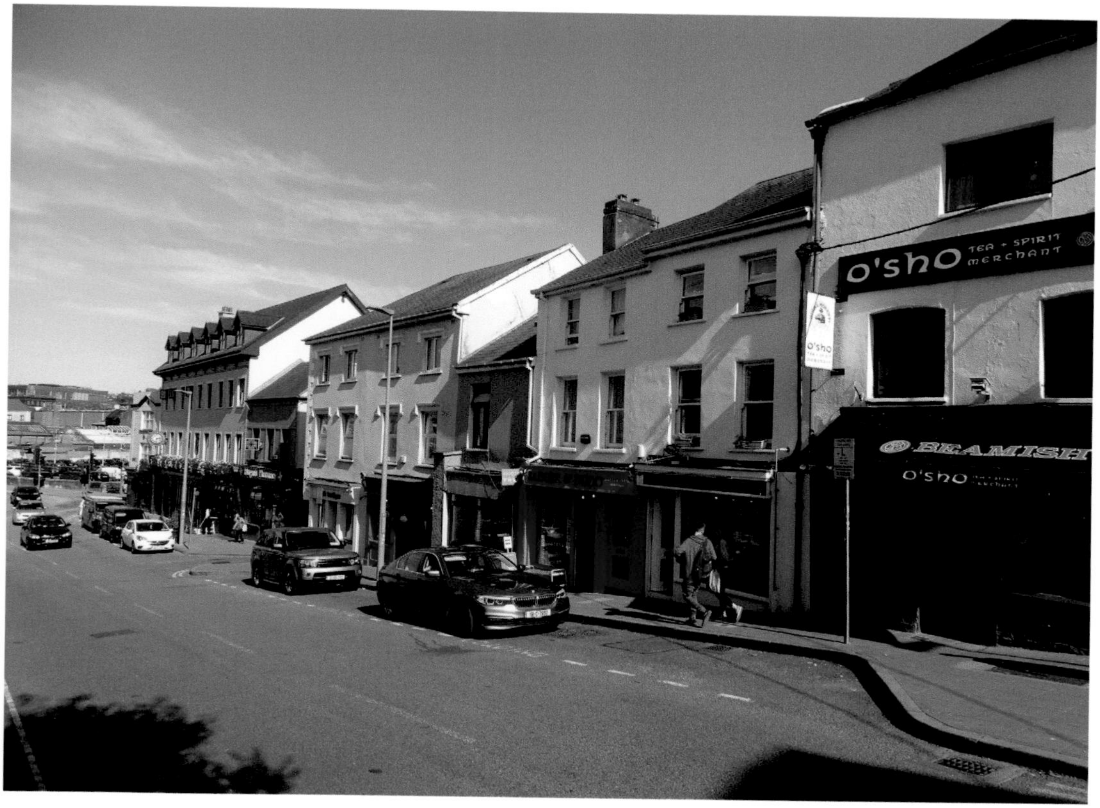

Cove Street and Barrack Street junction.

portion of the hall would be completely burnt out. The strenuous efforts of the members of the fire brigade, however, soon brought it under control. After several hours, the flames were overcome and the fires subdued. While not successful in their attack, the Black and Tans returned in the morning of Sunday 12 December to light City Hall and were successful in its destruction at that point.

14

What's in a Painting? Nathaniel Grogan's South Gate Bridge

Archived in the collections of the Crawford Art Gallery is an evocative painting of South Gate Bridge in the closing decade of the eighteenth century by artist Nathaniel Grogan (*c.* 1740–1807). He discovered his talent as an artist as a young man, receiving some instruction from the artist John Butts. Grogan enlisted in the British army and went to America for a time. He returned to Cork and became known for his composition skills of drawings of the city and its environs.

One of Grogan's popular works is that of South and North Gate Bridges. The image presented is that of South Gate Bridge, which reveals quite a lot of the life and times in this corner of the city, especially in its focus on the bridge, the debtor's prison and the fishing community.

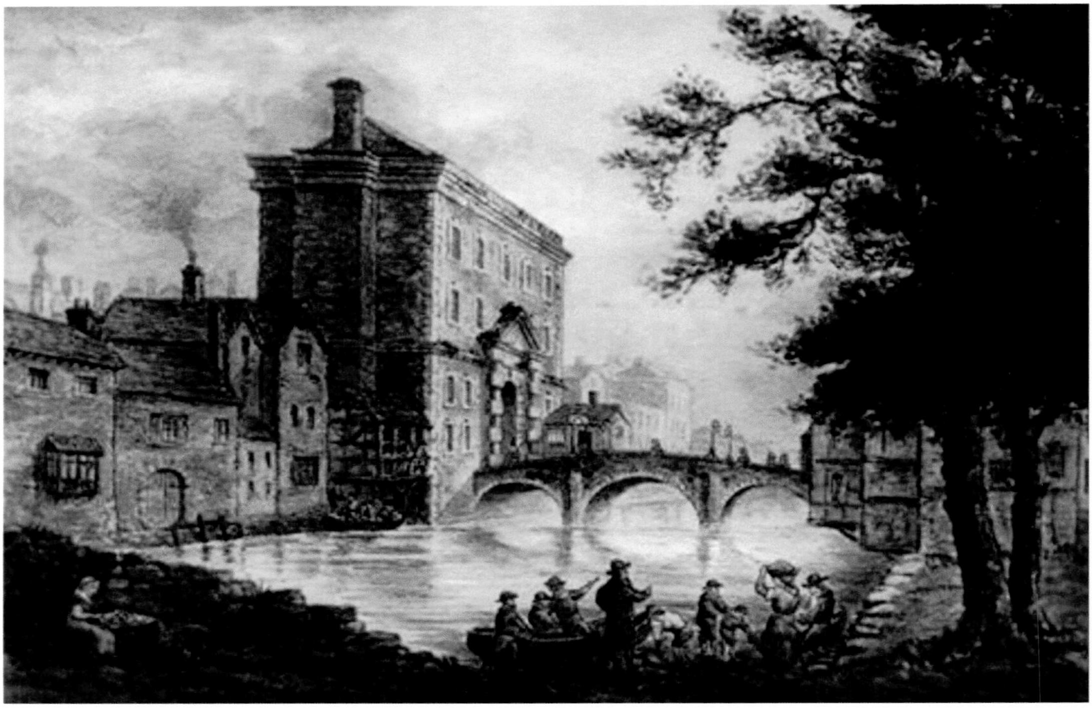

South Gate Bridge by Nathaniel Grogan, *c.* 1790. (Courtesy of Crawford Art Gallery)

It is said that the first South Gate Bridge was built sometime in the twelfth century AD as a timber-planked structure, giving access to a Hiberno Norse settlement or access to a well-settled marshland with inhabitants of Viking descendancy. When the Anglo-Normans established a fortified walled settlement and a trading centre in Cork around AD 1200, South Gate drawbridge formed one of the three entrances – North Gate drawbridge and Watergate portcullis being the others.

In May 1711, agreement was reached by the Corporation of Cork that North Gate Bridge would be rebuilt in stone, while in 1713 South Gate Bridge would be replaced with an arched stone structure. South Gate Bridge still stands today in the same form it did over 300 years ago, with the exception of a small bit of restructuring and re-strengthening in early 1994.

In the painting, the Debtor's Prison at South Gate Prison is very prominent, with its peaked roof and chimney piece at the left-hand side of the bridge. It is known the prison was built concurrent to the bridge in the 1710s. However, many of its records have been lost to time. What is known is that there were stern penalties if you owed money and could not pay the debt in eighteenth- and nineteenth-century Ireland. The debtor was imprisoned until the money was paid. If they did not have enough money to pay the debt, then it was not unusual for the person to remain in the prison until they died there.

Debtors were not entitled to medical attention. Those who could not get their families to arrange payments of rent at the prison had to take the dampest and darkest cells. If payment was not made for food, they were given bread that was boiled in water three times a day.

The practice of imprisoning debtors caused many to call for the reform of laws around debt. It was only in 1872 that the imprisonment aspect was removed by the Debtors Act (Ireland).

In the foreground of the painting there is a focus on fishermen. Records reveal that such fishermen lived around the Frenches Quay, Crosses Green and South Main Street areas. Several resided in the stepped lane known as Keyser's Hill that runs from Frenches Quay to Barrack Street via Elizabeth Fort. Twentieth-century oral history records that the South Parish fishermen used sturdy open rowing boats, usually around 18 feet in length. The boats were heavy and required considerable strength to row.

15

Beneath the Grand Parade City Car Park

In 2003 and 2004, large sections of the Grand Parade City Car Park were archaeologically excavated ahead of a development by Messrs Kenny Homes Ltd (it has not progressed to date). The excavations were directed by Máire Ní Loinsigh and Deborah Sutton of Sheila Lane & Associates.

The subsequent published archaeological report records many exciting finds. Among them was a total of 50.3 metres of Cork's town wall in length being discovered. The structure ran parallel to the existing riverside wall.

In general, much of the town wall survives beneath the modern street surface of the city and in some places has been incorporated into the foundations of existing buildings, in particular buildings overlooking the Grand Parade. Limestone and sandstone were used to construct the wall – both quarried locally.

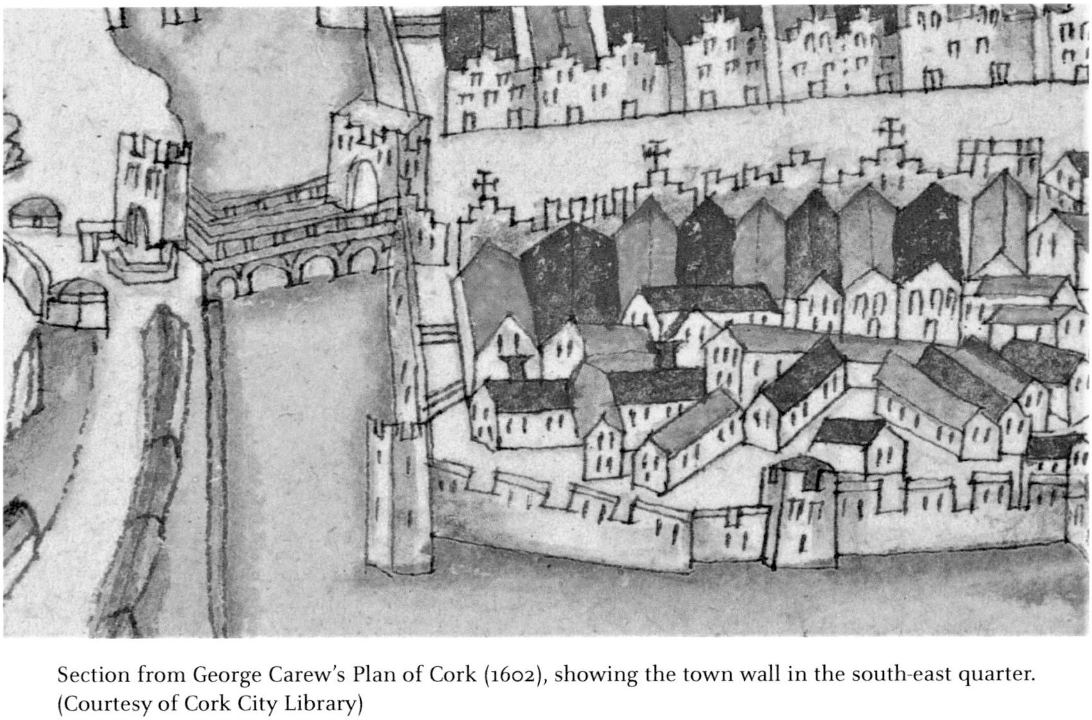

Section from George Carew's Plan of Cork (1602), showing the town wall in the south-east quarter. (Courtesy of Cork City Library)

The stone was cut into irregular-shaped blocks. Mortar has also been found between these blocks and an analysis of this has revealed that it was comprised of crushed eggshells and charcoal mixed in with gritty lime mortar, which held the blocks together.

Cork was one of fifty-eight walled towns in Ireland. Initially created by the Anglo-Normans, *c.* AD 1180, the town walls of Cork were extended and rebuilt by further English colonialists through subsequent centuries up to the Siege of Cork in 1690.

This section of the town wall discovered under the car park was part of the southern circuit of Cork's enclosing medieval wall, and on George Carew's Map of Cork it shows a large entrance (maybe a quayside?) of some kind embedded in it.

In some parts the wall was only 1 metre wide and it rarely exceeded 1.5 metres in width. The wall was constructed on a timber raft foundation. The town wall is described as being built of mortared stone on a 'single course of offset sandstone foundation slabs'.

The archaeologists discovered intentional dumping of waste to the north of the town wall, artificially raising the ground level. This was pursued to enable the building of the upper levels of the wall. Several rebuilds of the town wall were recorded.

What can also be seen in the Grand Parade building boundaries of the car park are the remains of arches of Lane's Brewery, which was opened in 1750 and closed in 1901.

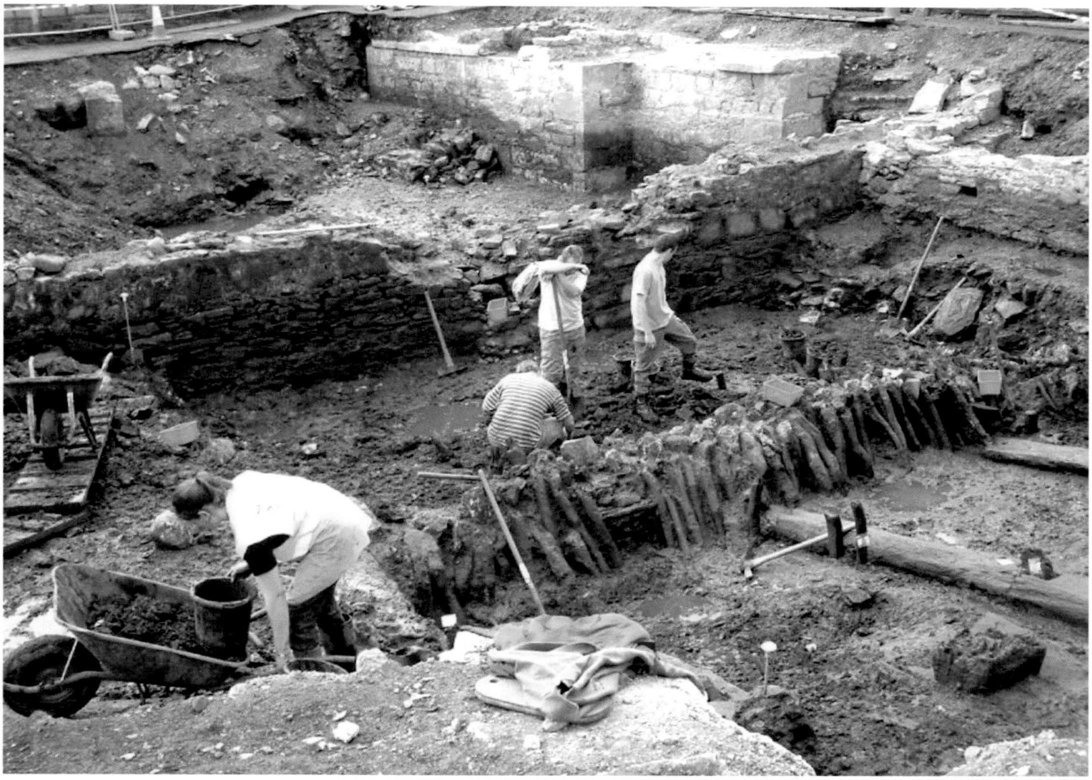

Excavations in June 2002 at Grand Parade City Car Park. The picture shows the town wall find and other medieval and post-medieval structures.

16

The Counting House

Founded in 1792 by William Beamish and William Crawford, the brewery became a huge success, and within a decade the company could boast it had sold 100,000 barrels of beer. Its principal industrial base was clustered around the curving River Lee adjacent South Gate Bridge. Increased competition though over the ensuing century almost halved output. In 1918, the company recorded an output of 59,326 barrels and an annual net profit averaging £45,236. Following the conclusion of the war, the management of the brewery commenced a number of projects to increase trade and to improve the reputation and image of the business.

In 1918 the architectural firm Chillingworth & Levie were employed to come up with designs of two of the firm's public houses – the Sextant Bar, Albert Street, and the Oval Bar on South Main Street. Such pubs were then to be houses under management rather than houses let to tenants. Both houses were to be places where products could be enjoyed in the best condition and in cosy spaces.

In 1919, Chillingworth and Levie were also employed to create plans for a new brewery office building that would present a rooted heritage in the city and a more attractive entrance to the more industrial buildings behind. Called the Counting House, it exterior possessed a Tudor Revival-style half-timbering complete with Tudor-style windows and hood mouldings. Inside was a public foyer, board room and offices.

The architectural partnership of Robert Chillingworth and Daniel Levie was apparently formed in 1911 and they had their offices at No. 11 South Mall, Cork. Certainly, the Beamish and Crawford contracts were some of their first larger design projects and possibly led

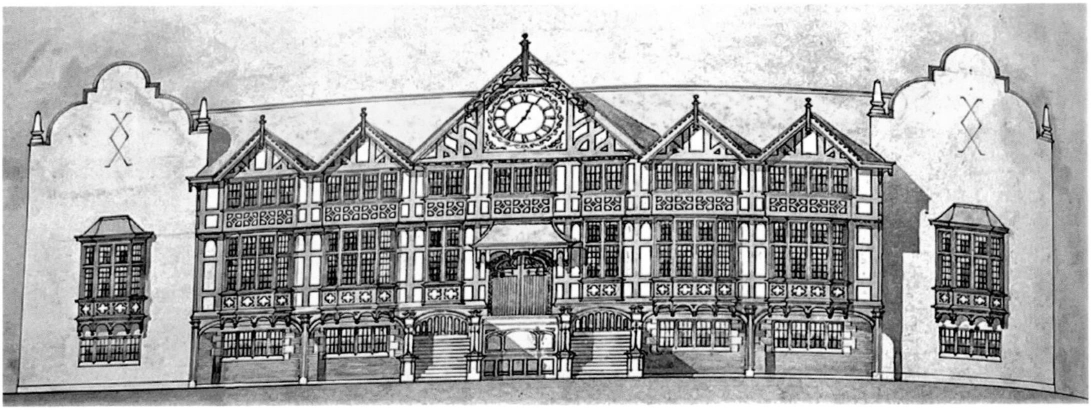

Plans by Chillingworth and Levie on the Counting House of Beamish and Crawford Brewery, South Main Street, 1919. (Courtesy of Cork City and County Archives)

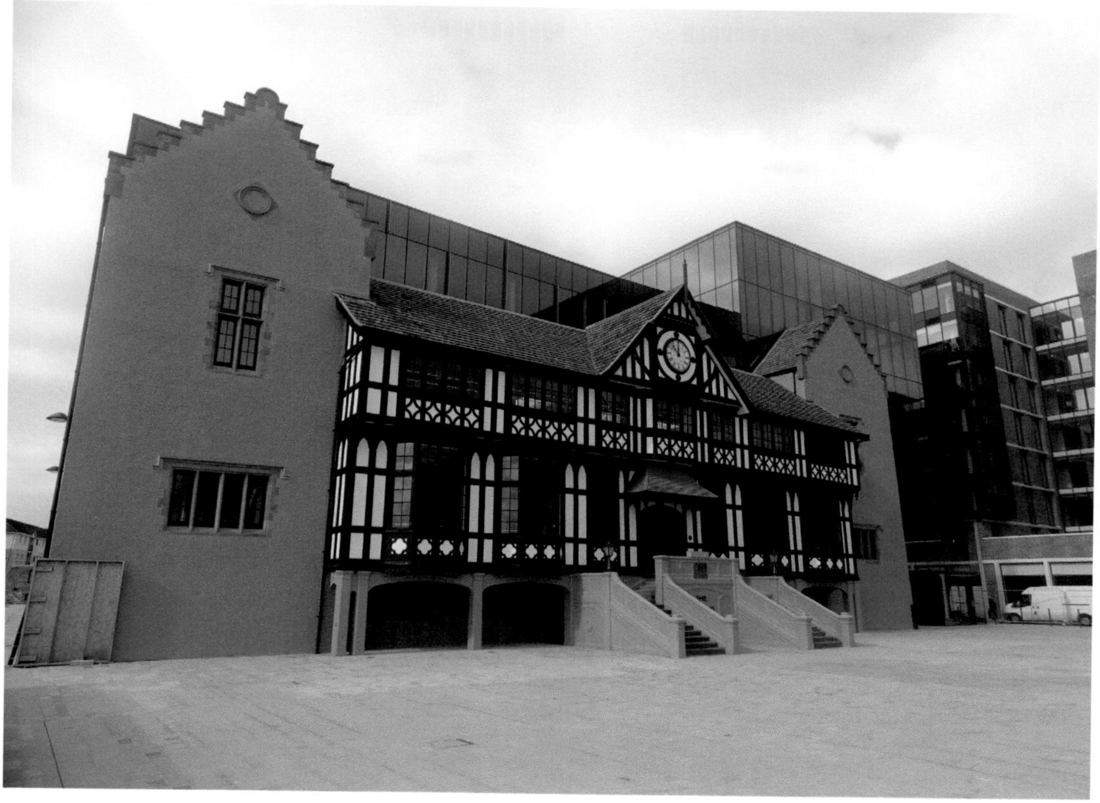

Former Counting House of Beamish and Crawford Brewery.

to being architects on a number of reconstruction projects on St Patrick's Street after the 'Burning of Cork' in 1920. The firm's impressive collection of drawings was saved from a building skip in 1986. It was then acquired by the Crawford Art Gallery and was transferred in 1988 to the Cork City and County Archives.

In recent years, the Counting Houses has been restored as part of a new 7,000-square-foot European-style public plaza, 70,000 square feet of 'best-in-class' office space, a 'cultural corridor' and the reinstatement of two old medieval laneways – all part of a massive €30 million regeneration of Cork city's medieval quarter. The clock mechanism was repaired by Stokes Clocks and Watches Ltd, Cork.

17

The Crypt of Christ Church

Christ Church, now the Triskel Christ Church Arts Centre, is reputed to be the third significant building on the site. The first church was Danish and the second building was Anglo-Norman. The Normans came and took possession of Cork in 1177 and in 1180, and Christ Church was rebuilt as a stone structure on the same site as the first. The second church comprised a tower, a steeple, a peal of bells and thick walls. Encompassing the church was a college, almshouse, gardens and houses for the priests.

A chapel in praise of the Crusades was built in 1310. An organ was given by Sir Francis Drake to the church, which he took from a Spanish Galleon *c.* 1588. During the Siege of Cork in 1690, supporters of James II took over the walled city, captured some Protestant inhabitants and shut them in the tower of Christ Church. Christ Church was badly damaged by a cannonball in the siege, which landed on the roof and destroyed it.

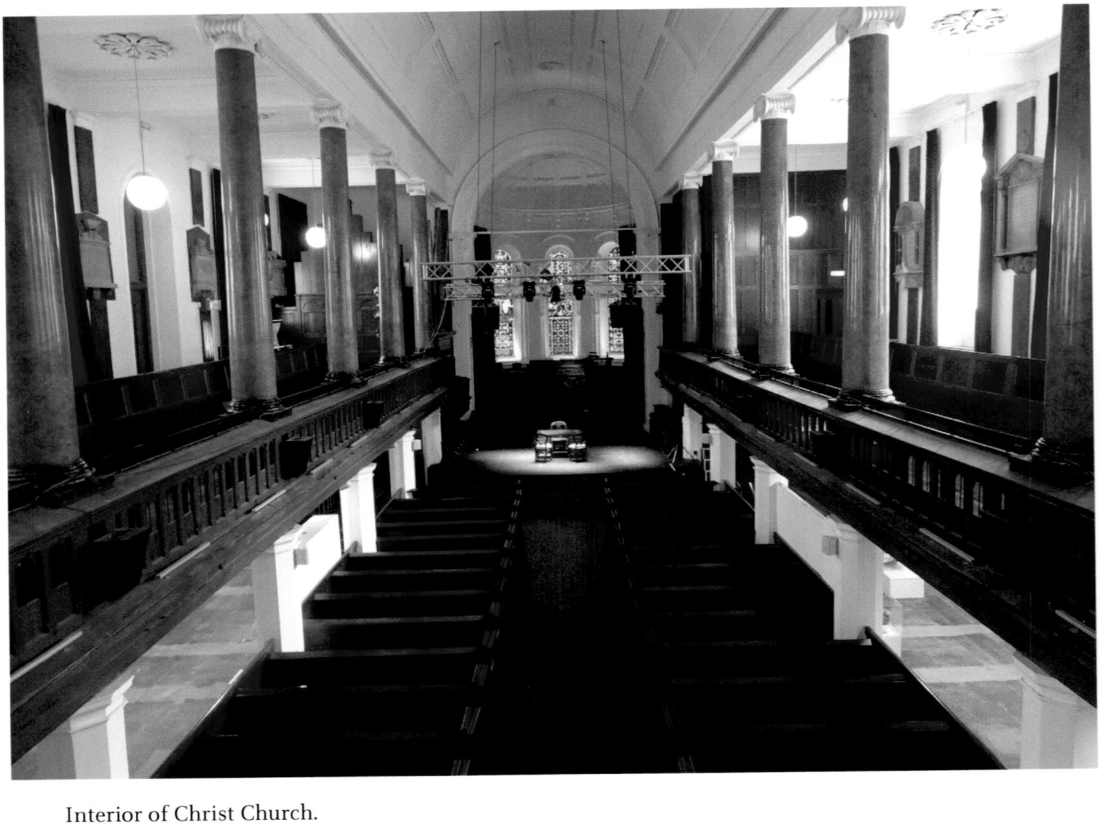

Interior of Christ Church.

The third church was then built and the first sermon was preached from its pulpit by Revd Philip Townsend on 20 November 1720. The church was rebuilt by George Coltsman, who also designed the eighteenth-century South Gate and North Gate Bridges and their associated gaolhouses. Disaster struck in the new western tower when its foundation sank, making it lean. Over the centuries, various renovations have been carried out to reduce the slope of the leaning tower. Be sure to check out former mayor of Cork Thomas Ronan's Modest Man tombstone and the crypt beneath the church.

On a visit to Christ Church one can also visit the crypt. Interpretative material highlights that it was constructed in 1718–20, after the knocking down of the old Anglo-Norman church. The floor level of the crypt (as it one sees now) may have been the floor level of this church. Several of the leading merchant families of Cork are buried in the crypt, including a number of former mayors.

The crypt comprises one narrow and three wide aisles running on an east–west axis beneath the church. Burials within crypts were largely not interred, but the wooden and metal coffins were assembled in locked chambers within vaults. During the 2009 renovation of Christchurch part of the crypt wall of the church was removed and a glass viewing box was created.

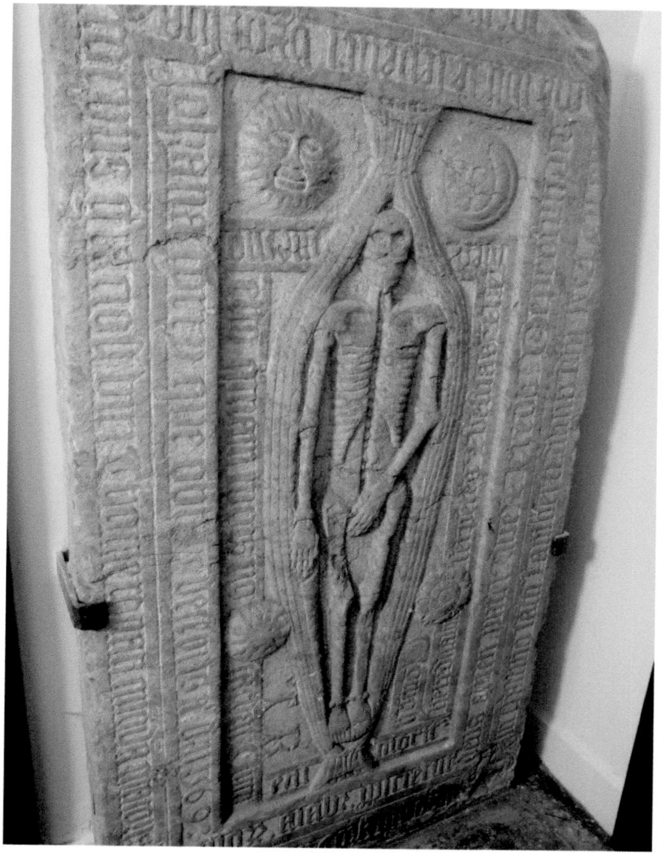

The Modest Man, Christ Church.

18

The Tuckeys of Tuckey Street

The first member of the Quaker Tuckey family arrived in Cork in Oliver Cromwell's army. A leading figure in the parish of Christ Church, Timothy Tuckey Sr died in 1668 and was interred in a vault in the church's crypt. Tuckey's son Timothy was elected Mayor of Cork in 1677, and it is after him the lane and subsequent street was named.

The damage from the Siege of Cork in 1690 was significant: the town walls lay heavily broken down and houses had been razed to the ground. The decision to take down the town walls and leave the town to expand on marshes was not taken lightly, and it was a process that took fifty years. The Tuckey family were leaders in this regard.

Around 1694, Ormond's Quay outside the town wall was leased to Alderman Timothy Tuckey for ninety-nine years at a yearly rent of 11*s*. It became formally known as Tuckey's Quay and is now the City Library footpath section of the Grand Parade to Tuckey Street. A year later, in 1695, Timothy Tuckey was given liberty to build houses on the quay providing he left 20 feet clear in breath of the quay. Over the ensuing ten years, Timothy Tuckey also took down several sections of the town wall to its foundations.

One particular and significant venture, which was recorded at length in Cork Corporation's council books, was the agreement between Alderman Tuckey and the

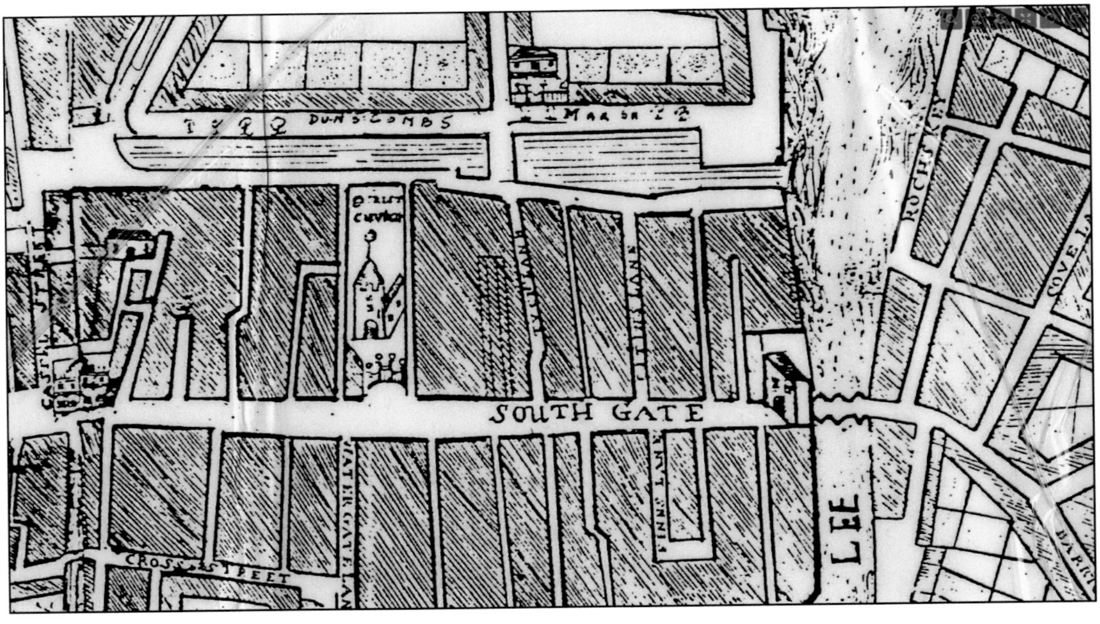

Plan of Tuckey Street from John Carty's Map of Cork, 1726. (Courtesy of Cork City Library)

Dunscombe Quaker family in 1698. In mid-January 1698, Captain Dunscombe was given liberty to build a stone bridge from Tuckey's quay onto his leased marsh. The Corporation of Cork required that the new bridge have arches high and broad enough for a small boat to pass under at high tide and must be kept in repair by the Dunscombe family and their heirs. Berwick Fountain is the exact site of Tuckey's Bridge, which spanned a canal at that place, and on which an equestrian statue of George II was first erected.

As for Tuckey's Lane, it was widened in 1761. Check out the inscribed limestone plaque on the street.

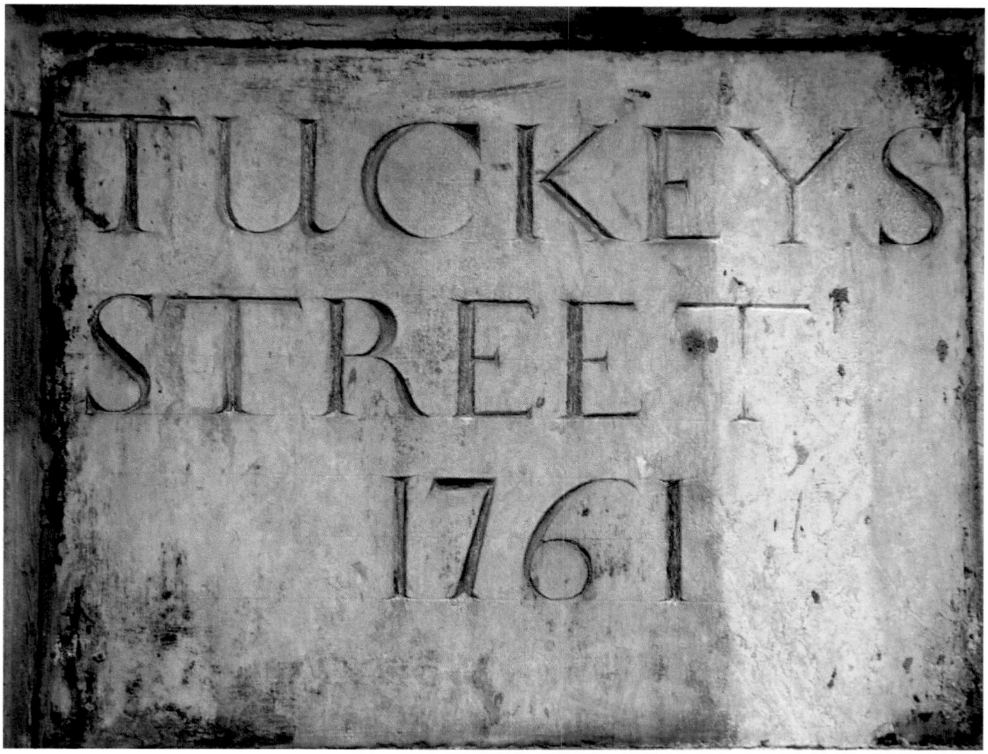

Plaque denoting the widening of Tuckey Street in 1761.

19

Washington Street and the Wide Street Commissioners

As the late eighteenth century progressed, the population increased and the Corporation of Cork came under pressure to improve the lives of citizens. The medieval fabric of the city simply could not cope with the demands of the population. Fines were placed on illegal dumping and scavengers, and wheelbarrow men and street sweepers were appointed to keep the streets clean. Many of the buildings in the city were in need of much repair and certain lanes in the old medieval core needed to be reconstructed.

In 1765 a commission was established to deal with the problems facing the expanding city, especially in relation to the various health risks posed by inadequate facilities. Known as the Wide Street Commission, it was first set up in Dublin. In Cork, its primary job was to widen the medieval lanes and thereby eradicate some of the health problems stemming from them. They also planned to lay out new, wider streets for the benefit of the citizens.

Sixteen commissioners were appointed in 1765, but due to financial restrictions it was the early nineteenth century before they made an impact. At that time, streets such as South Terrace, Dunbar Street and Washington Street (then known as Great George's

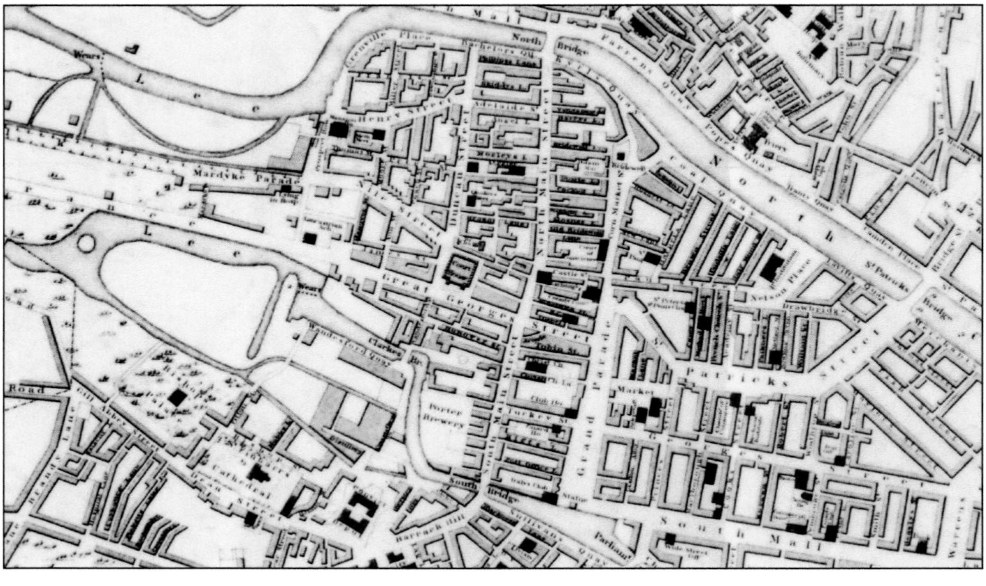

Section of Holt's Map of Cork (1832), showing Great George Street. (Courtesy of Cork City Library)

Street; opened in November 1824) were laid out, and streets such as Shandon Street were widened.

Samuel Lewis, in his section on Cork in his *Topographical Dictionary of Ireland* (1837), describes the work of the commissioners: 'The streets were created and repaired under the directions of the commissioners and nearly £6000 is annually expended in paving, cleansing, and improving them.' The privilege of licensing vehicles of every description plying for hire within the city was also vested in these commissioners.

Lewis describes that the general appearance of the city, particularly since its extensive improvements, is 'picturesque and cheerful'. He further outlines that 'the principal streets are spacious and well paved; most of the houses are large and well built, chiefly of clay-slate fronted with roofing slate, which gives them a clean though sombre appearance; others are built of the beautiful grey limestone of the neighbourhood, and some are faced with cement; those in the new streets are principally of red brick'.

John Windele, in his *Historical and Descriptive Notices of Cork* (1849), describes a dense habitation prior to Great George's Street: 'The sight of this beautiful street a few years ago was occupied by some of the narrowest and filthiest lanes and alleys of the town and most densely inhabited by a squalid and impoverished population.'

On 21 September 1824, led by the mayor, the members of the Corporation of Cork paraded to the new street where they were greeted by the commissioners. The new street had been laid out to join the new road, which at the time was named the King's Road (now Western Road). As well as marking the official opening of the new street, the ceremonies in September 1824 also included laying the foundation and cornerstones of houses to be erected by the architects Thomas and Alexander Deane on the north side of the new street. Thomas Deane presented Mayor Bartholomew Gibbings with a silver trowel and the foundation and cornerstones were placed in position. The mayor then ceremoniously named the new street Great George's Street in honour of the reigning monarch, George IV.

Meanwhile, a memorial tablet on No. 4 Washington Street (West) tells the viewer that the foundation stone for the houses on the south side of the street was laid on 15 June 1827, which indicates that the Deane brothers were building up the street rapidly.

From the Grand Parade to Lancaster Quay, one can view an impressive run of terraced nineteenth-century buildings retaining their original scale, form as well as a roofline, consistent with the rest of the streetscape. Breaking the terrace's view at points are some of the city's most impressive nineteenth-century buildings.

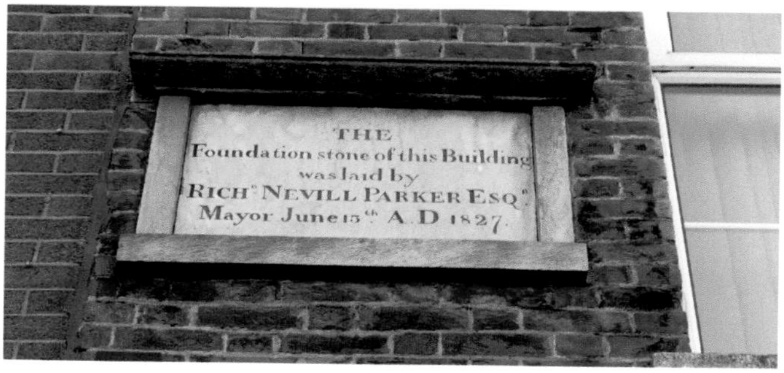

Memorial tablet at No. 4 Washington Street (West), 15 June 1827.

In 1829, it was decided by Cork Corporation that both the City and County Courthouses should be incorporated into one building, to be located on the new Great George's Street on the old western line of the town wall. Designed by George Pain, the courthouse was built on the western line of the old town wall and opened in 1835. Years later, on Good Friday 27 March 1891, the interior was completely destroyed by fire. William Henry Hill was chosen to oversee the reconstruction of the building.

In 1835, a terraced four-bay four-storey terraced premises belonging to Messrs John Reardan and Sons was to be used as public house. In 1892, Stratten and Stratten's *Dublin, Cork and South of Ireland* (a commercial directory) outline that the firm's wine stores were situated at Lancaster Quay and Wood's Lane, where they also have a stock of 200–300 casks of cider, while the bonded store was at No. 14, Custom House. Today the bar is still thriving and famous across Ireland as Cork's largest bar venue for live music and entertainment.

Around 1840, an impressive three-storey premises was added to the street on a very distinctive triangular site. Its triangular plan tapering to a bullnose corner is notable.

In 1874, a fine example of a nineteenth-century commercial building – a nine-bay, four-storey Venetian-style building – was constructed to house the House of Dwyer. Between the 1820s and the 1980s, from their base at Nos 26–29 Washington Street, the Dwyers created a business empire that employed thousands of people in a manufacturing company that included such names as the Lee Boot Factory and Hanover Shoes, Sunbeam Wolsey, Perdix Shirts and Knitwear, Seafield Gentex, and Templemichael Mills.

The name Dwyers is woven into the fabric of Cork, beginning in 1820 with James Dwyer establishing a drapery, wholesale and haberdashery business on Washington Street. Over the next century the enterprise grew into an empire that employed thousands, Dwyer and his descendants striding tall among the 'merchant princes' of the city. The building now hosts Dwyers of Cork Restaurant and the Courthouse Chambers.

On Friday 27 September 1918, Cork Corporation resolved that Great Georges and Great George Street West should henceforth be deemed one street and be renamed Washington Street. This was a compliment to America and emphasised and commemorated the part played by Irish people, backed by the sympathy and support of the Irish diaspora, in the American War of Independence.

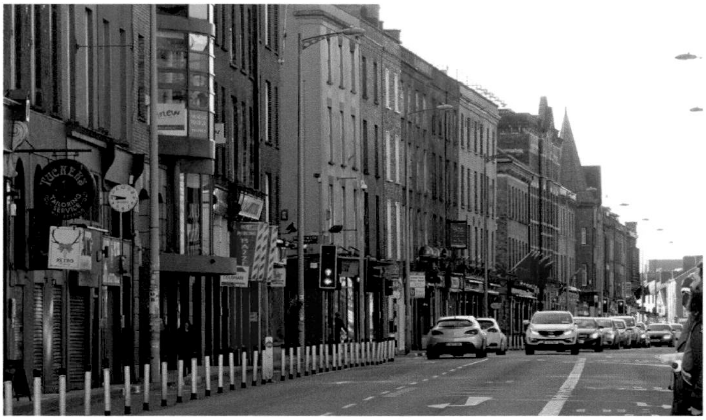

Washington Street.

20

The King's Castle

The Watergate complex, comprising Cork's medieval port, docks and customs house, would have been impressive. The gate allowed controlled access into a private world of merchants and citizens. Built between two marshy islands, in the middle of a walled town, its entrance was between the two castles – King's Castle and Queen's Castle. King's and Queen's Castles are signified in the city's coat of arms with a ship travelling from one tower to another and the Latin inscription *Statio Bene Fida Carinis*, which means 'A Safe Harbour for Ships'.

In the early seventeenth century the lower part of King's Castle was converted in two: the county prison below and the upper floor was used as the County Courthouse.

In 1680 a new purpose-built courthouse was constructed. It was described as a plain, accommodating structure with grand jury rooms. In 1806 a further new courthouse was constructed on the site and was renamed King's Old Castle. It consisted of a handsome parliament of Portland stone supported by fluted Doric columns resting on a rustic basement. The cost of building was £10,000.

After the erection of the new courthouse on great George's Street, these premises were no longer required for the County Court services. The building passed into the possession of William Fitzgibbon, who established the Queen's Old Castle. The name was a compliment to Queen Victoria, the then reigning monarch.

William Fitzgibbon was a native of Rathkeale, County Limerick. His first drapery store was in Cork's Mallow Lane, now Shandon Street, and proved a great success. After a few years he transferred the business to Great George's Street and assembled, bit by bit, leaseholds and simple properties, including the disused Cork Courthouse. In 1846 the new drapery warehouse was ready for occupation. Space 1 was the first fully equipped

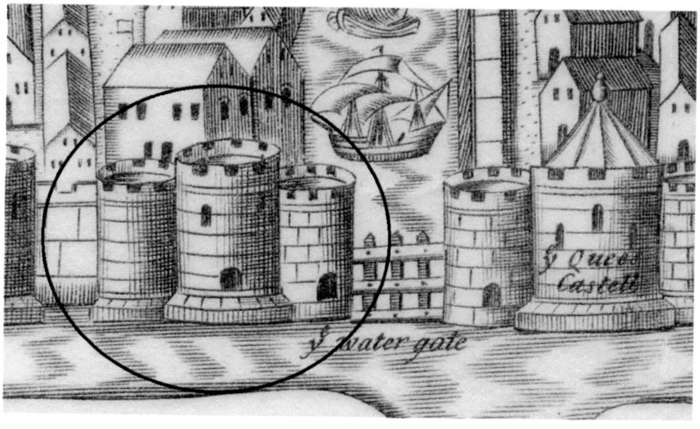

Sketch of King's Castle *c.* 1600 from George Carew's *Pacata Hibernia*. (Courtesy of Cork City Library)

monster drapery warehouse in the United Kingdom. It was one of the most popular department stores in Cork.

In 1873 Mr Victor Beare Fitzgibbon of Queen's Old Castle, Messrs Alexander Grant and T. Lyons merged the three business into a limited liability company under the title of T. Lyons and Co. Limited, and focussed on the Queen's Old Castle warehouse. The three businesses formed the principal members of the directorate. They established a trade that, in point of magnitude and volume, had never before been equalled in the annals of commercial enterprise in the South of Ireland. All three firms also continued their respective operations.

The Queen's Old Castle survived the 'Burning of Cork' in 1920. In 1928 renovation works were entrusted to the firm of Mr T. Kelleher, Millerd Street, with architectural drawings by Messrs Chillingworth and Levie. Changes included the old shopfront being completely removed as well as the heavy masonry piers that supported the Portland stone columns.

There was further change in 1996 when Clarendon Properties bought the building. It closed for refurbishment and when it reopened there were just two main tenants – catalogue retailer Argos and Virgin Music Megastore. Both stores have since closed and a Dealz is the only business currently occupying the site.

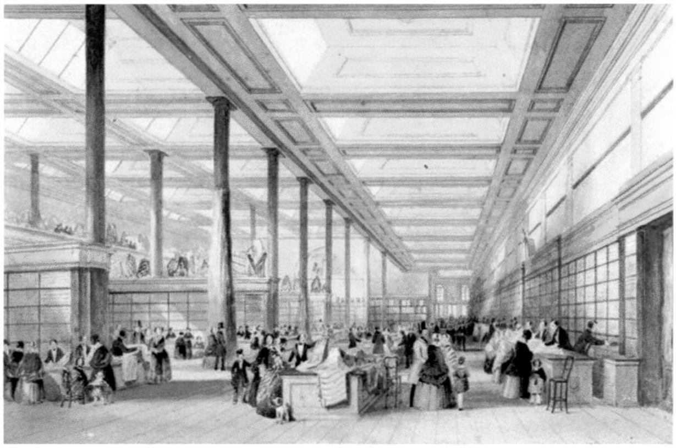

Robert Lowe Stopford's watercolour of the interior of the Queen's Old Castle, Cork, 1848. (Courtesy of Crawford Art Gallery)

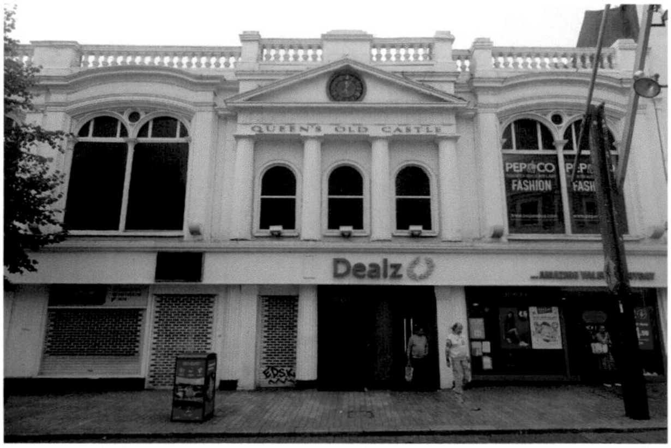

Queen's Old Castle.

21

The Quaker Meeting House

The impact of the Quaker community in Cork is documented primarily by local historian Richard Harrison (*c.* 1985 and 1999). He outlines their arrival in Cork and how select individuals of prominent families, such as the Pikes, Quakers and Hamans, were responsible in physically developing much of the marshes to the immediate west of the walled town of Cork.

In Cork, the first Quakers settled in the town in 1655 when Elizabeth Fletcher and Elizabeth Smith arrived to take up residence. The first church was on a laneway off North Main Street, near the town cross, on North Main. The laneway has a bronze plaque.

By the late 1690s, the Quaker movement were able to consolidate themselves further in Cork Society when the Corporation of Cork accepted and acknowledged the religion's presence. This was due to the fact that the Quakers could financially aid the Corporation out of debt. Hence, between 1690 and 1700, several prominent members of the Cork Quaker community were made freemen by the Corporation and accepted into trade guilds.

The first freeman included Ebenezer Pike and Richard Pike. Richard Pike was in partnership with William Alloway, who established the first linen drapery in Cork. Richard's father, Joseph Pike, initially dealt in wool and English goods but when the English Parliament outlawed the export of serge to the Continent he turned to the export of Bay yarn to England.

In 1696, Joseph Pike became one of the first Quakers in Cork to pioneer the investment of capital into reclaiming marshland in order to create residences. In that year, he purchased a large portion of an unnamed marshy island just to the west of the walled town.

Other Quaker families soon followed the Pike investment. The Fenn family leased the land from the Pikes in 1705. John Haman, a respected linen merchant, also reclaimed land for residential purposes. He also bought land in the north-western suburbs of the town in the first decade of the 1700s. Other families that invested in land in the early decades of the 1700s were the Devonshire and the Sleigh families respectively.

All of those names mentioned named the marshes after themselves. A good example is Fenn's Marsh. The name Fenn still resonates on the present-day townscape in the form of the street Fenn's Quay, which in the early 1700s was built adjacent a channel of the River Lee.

Apart from developing land, individual Quakers also recognised that the town's people were in need of finance and offered their service as private bankers. Brothers Edward and Joseph Hoare established the first private bank in 1675. Joseph was married to Rachel Rogers, whose sister was married to Joseph Pike. In 1720, Joseph Pike became a partner of the Hoare Bank, and after both brothers died in the 1720s it was the Pike family that continued on the banking tradition in Cork well into the nineteenth century.

The sixteenth-century Quaker meeting house was replaced at least twice – first in 1777 and then in 1833. The 1833 meeting house was designed by architect

G. T. Beale – an ornate, detached, six-bay, two-storey building on Grattan Street. In 1939, a smaller meeting house was built on Summerhill South adjacent to their early eighteenth-century graveyard. The Quaker movement also established itself in Bandon, Skibbereen, Charleville and Youghal.

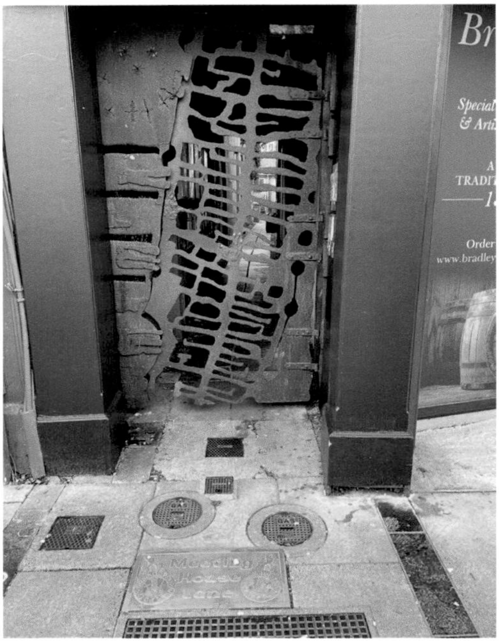

Left: Meeting House Lane on North Main Street.

Below: The 1833 meeting house designed by architect G. T. Beale – an ornate, detached, six-bay, two-storey building on Grattan Street, now the offices of the HSE.

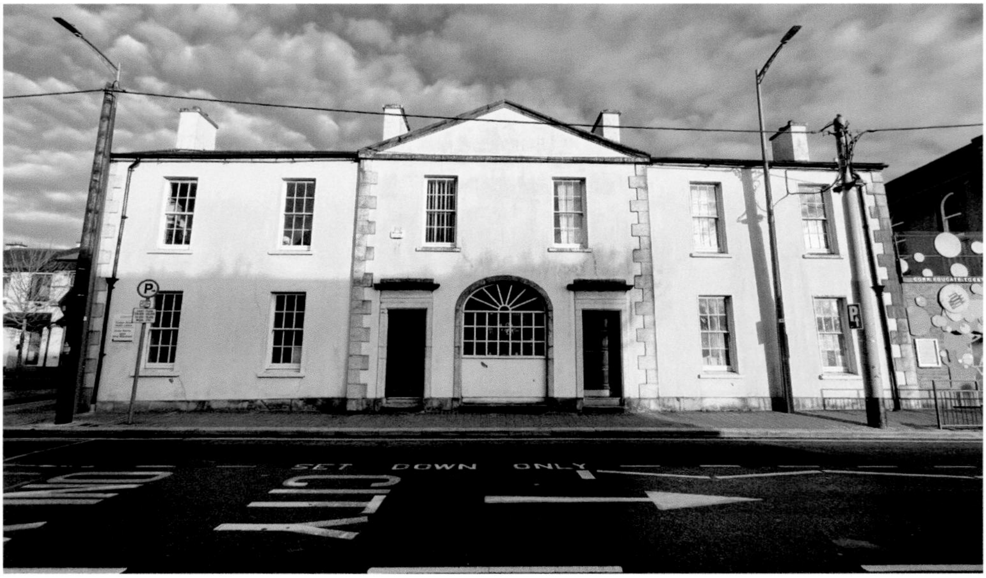

22

In Context, North Main Street

Today, if you walk through North Main Street, you can see clearly the building fabric dating between 1820 and 1850, and there is a clear strategy to build over some of the historic lanes in the city. However, beneath the streets lies its medieval past. It is well documented that from the early stages of the Anglo-Norman arrival that the topography of the marshy islands began to change. The Hiberno Norse settlement on the southern marshy island, or the marshland, which began to be developed was taken for the king by Milo de Cogan and Robert Fitzstephen and fortified. By 1300 a large stone wall – on average 8 metres high – enclosed the southern marshy island. It is also suggested that an unenclosed settlement developed just outside the southern island to the north on what is described by Cork historians as the northern island. Documentary sources detail the island to be a suburb of the fortification on the southern island. This suburb was more generally known as Dungarvan.

In a historical sense, the name Dungarvan means Garvan's Fort, but there is no real documentary evidence to back up the existence of a fort on this island. It is thought that the southern marshy island was connected to the northern island via a bridge. This is due to the fact that in 1199 a charter by Richard de Careu granting land to St Thomas Abbey in Dublin recorded the existence of a bridge between the city (southern island) and Dungarvan (northern Island).

Two historic municipal charters specify the granting of land to a religious institution and state a bridge existed that connected Dungarvan to the northern hillside overlooking the walled town. Philip de Barry's grant of land was made up of two plots and was located next to the bridge of Dungarvan. He gave this to St Thomas Abbey in Dublin. In 1182 Anglo-Norman lords Milo de Cogan and Robert Fitzstephen sent documentation to St Thomas Abbey in Dublin, which outlined that a mill of some sort also existed between the south island and Dungarvan.

In an archaeological sense, three excavations in the last forty years have revealed evidence for the existence of Dungarvan. Firstly, between October 1983 and January 1984, excavations by archaeologist Maurice Hurley and his team at St Peter's Market, Cornmarket Street, revealed the remains of a mural turret which was suggested as being built in the mid-thirteenth century and abandoned by the late thirteenth century.

Secondly, in 1994, excavations again by archaeologist Maurice Hurley and his team on the eastern side of North Main Street, now the site of a shopping centre, uncovered a quay wall in mid-thirteenth-century deposits. The wall itself was suggested as being a quay wall for the suburb of Dungarvan. The excavation report details that the wall itself was built of irregularly shaped blocks of mainly red sandstone on its outer face which overlooked the river and green sandstone on its inner face looking onto northern island.

In 1997, excavations by archaeologist Catyrn Power and her team on North Main Street revealed parts of a suggested raft foundation for a wooden road. The timbers were dated to the twelfth century and may have belonged to the initial settlement on the southern island or to a settlement on Dungarvan or the northern island. Adjacent to this medieval road lay possible fronts of timber houses were found which also dated to the twelfth century.

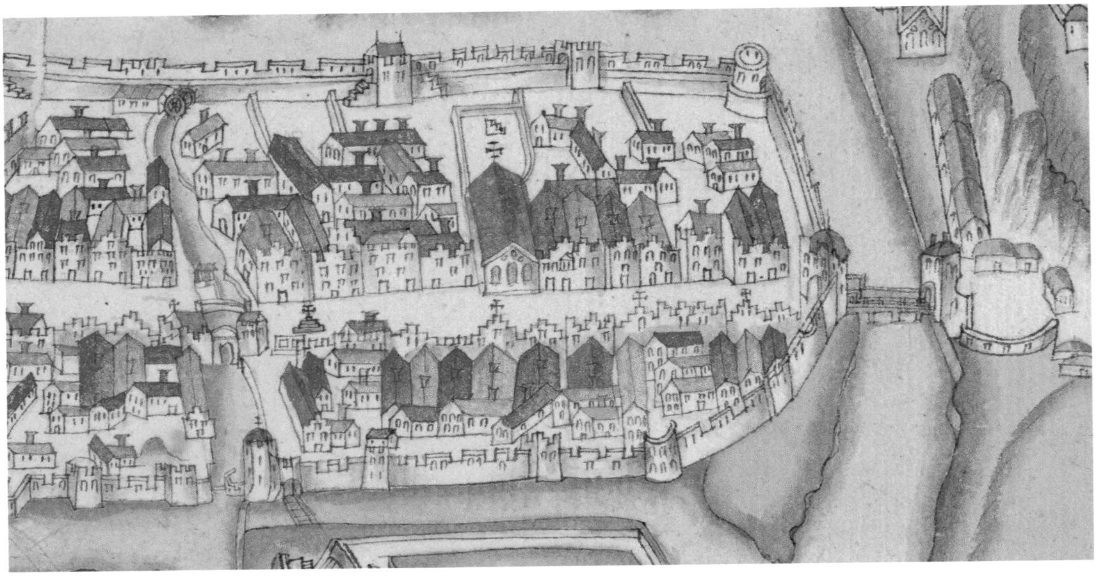

Sketch of North Main Street from George Carew's Map of Cork, *c.* 1601. (Courtesy of Cork City Library)

23

St Peter's Church

Present-day St Peter's Church is the second church to be built on its current site overlooking North Main Street. The first church was built sometime in the early fourteenth century. In 1782, the church was taken down, and in 1783 the present limestone-walled church had begun to be built. At a later stage, a new tower and spire were added to the basic rectangular plan. The new spire, though, had to be taken down due to the marshy ground that it was built on.

In recent years and in accordance with the aims of the pilot project of the Cork Historic Centre Action and the finance of Cork City Council and operational support of Cork Civic Trust, St Peter's Church has been extensively renovated and opened as an arts exhibition centre.

One of the most interesting monuments on display in the church is the Deane monument. This monument, dating to 1710, was dedicated to the memory of Sir Matthew Deane and his wife. Both are depicted on the monument, shown in solemn prayer on both sides of an altar tomb.

Now a deconsecrated space, a historic graveyard was attached to the medieval parish church of St Peter. The graveyard is in use as a public amenity space. In 1750, Charles Smith, in his *History of Cork* (1750), recorded that some of the gravestones had 'dates as old as the year 1500'.

Antiquarian John Windele records the discovery in 1838, of numerous tombstones belonging to the 'olden era of this Church, forming the foundations of the building which preceded its present steeple. shows to what uses the ancient remains connected with this building have been converted'. Certainly, the site has undergone modification and possibly significant disturbance to underlying deposits. Burials within the church would have been substantially dislocated during the demolition works of 1782 and the construction of the present church.

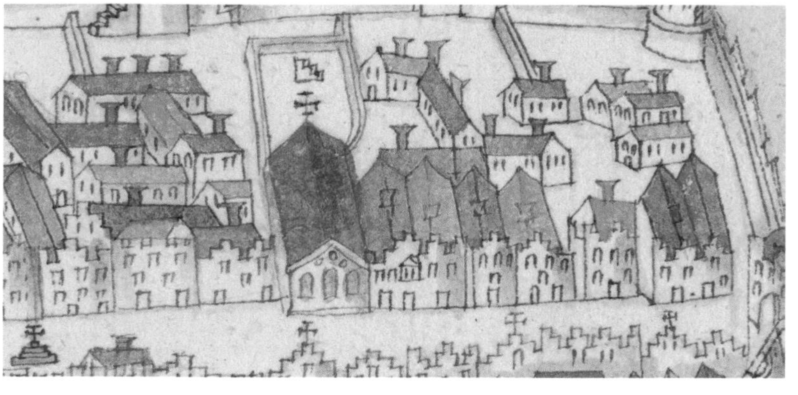

Sketch of St Peter' Church, North Main Street, from George Carew's Map of Cork, c. 1601. (Courtesy of Cork City Library)

During renovations to the church building during the 1990s, skeletal remains were uncovered beneath the floor.

Since 1975, Cork City Council has maintained the graveyard, which is when it was laid out as a park. There are thirteen headstones lining the northern boundary wall towards the back of the church. The headstones that are legible date to the eighteenth century. They are not in their original spot. The chest tomb of William Rogers (1686) also remains in its original position in the graveyard.

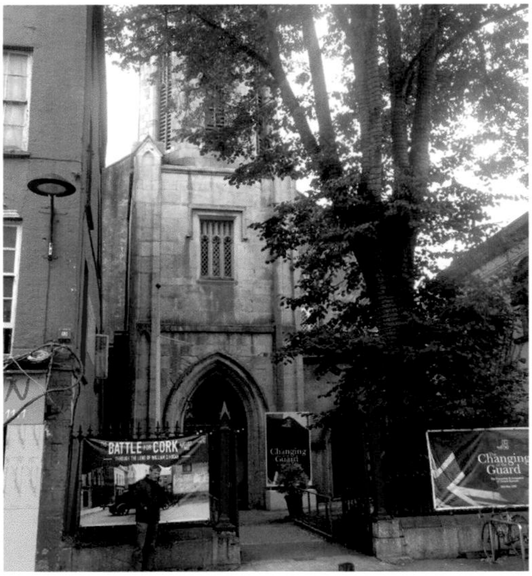

Left: St Peter's Church, North Main Street.

Below: Historic graveyard of St Peter's Church.

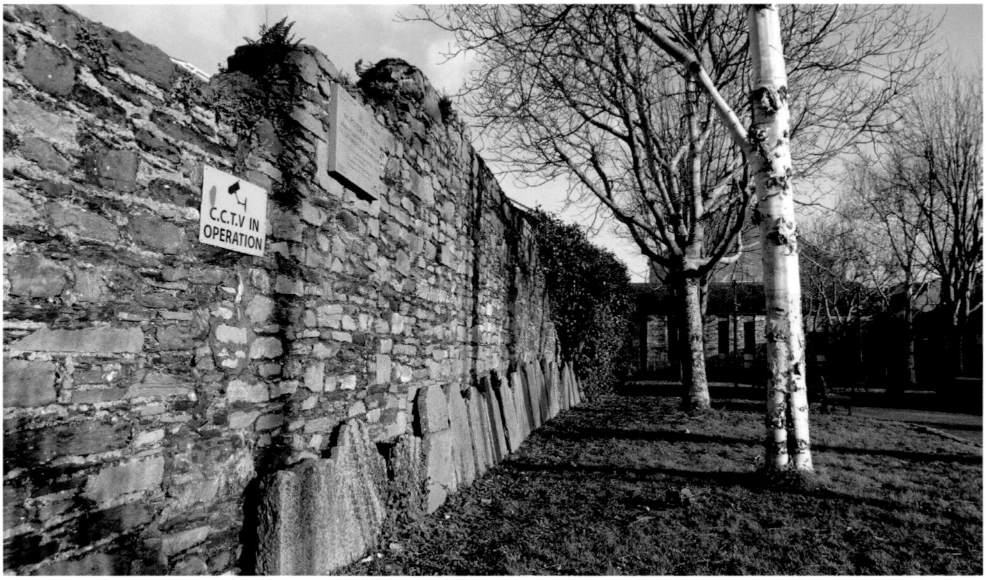

24

A Sixteenth-century Mantlepiece

George Carew's depiction of the walled town *c.* 1585–1600 shows two tower houses or castle-like structures on North Main Street. These residences – Skiddy's Castle and Roche's Castle – belonged to two wealthy and influential merchant families. The Skiddy family was reputedly descended from Scandinavian merchants who established themselves in Cork around 1445.

Skiddy's Castle was one of the most famous landmarks in the walled town of Cork. It was a tower house built in 1445 or 1447 by either John or William Skiddy. In 1603 the castle was taken over and used as a royal gunpowder magazine until 1770. The castle is shown on all the ancient maps of Cork, where it is depicted as both a round and a rectangular structure. No trace of the castle remains above ground.

In 1974, excavations by archaeologist Dermot Twohig and his team on North Main Street, in the area of what is now a public square at the intersection with Adelaide Street, revealed the base of Skiddy's Castle.

The ground-floor room survived almost intact beneath the modern surface. The plan was rectangular, and the room was divided in two by a partition. The walls stood to a height of almost 2 metres above a wooden raft. Pointed wooden stakes were used as piles to strengthen the foundations.

A 2-metre-high stone mantlepiece was found with the inscription '1597 G.S.' with floral motifs. The mantlepiece was incorporated into the Cork Volunteer Centre on North Main Street and placed high above the main entrance where it can still be seen.

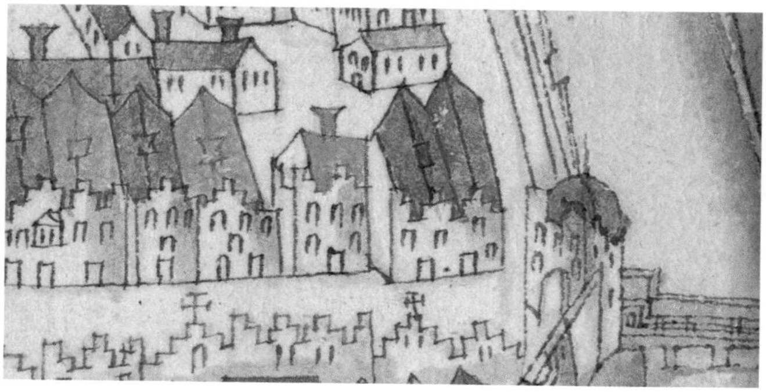

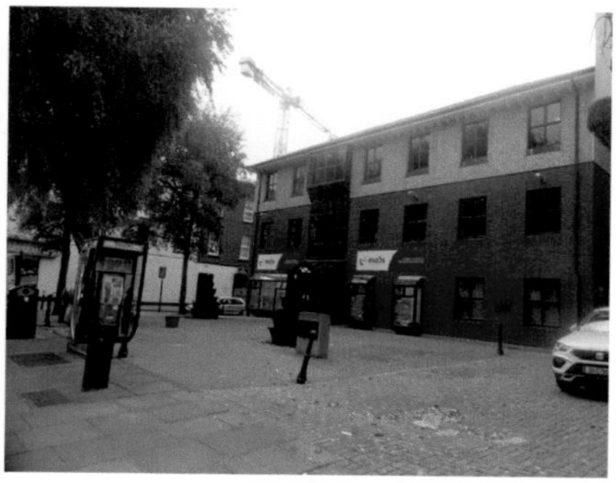

Above left: Sketch of Skiddy's Castle, North Main Street, from George Carew's Map of Cork, *c.* 1601. (Courtesy of Cork City Library)

Above right: Site of Skiddy's Castle.

25

The Kyrl's Quay Find

In May 1992, before redevelopment of the site as a multistorey car park and shopping centre, Cork Corporation, on behalf of the developer, conducted archaeological work under archaeologist Maurice Hurley and his team. A total of 580 square metres were completed by the beginning of July.

The earliest occupation levels explored were thirteenth century in date. No remains of medieval houses were discovered in the core section of the site, but discoveries on the post-and-wattle property boundaries of the burgess plots, as well as storage and cesspits, were present. For 800 years the property boundaries remained practically unaffected.

Adjacent to North Main Street the incomplete foundations of thirteenth-/fourteenth-century timber-framed houses were unearthed. Later, these houses were rebuilt in stone.

Most significantly, between July and September 60 metres of the town wall's length (north-east quarter) were excavated. The extant wall rose to a maximum height of 3.2 metres. It was mostly of thirteenth-century date but included some segments that were reconstructed at later times. Within the wall were two gateways. One had a paved slipway through which small boats could have been pulled up. Iron hinge pivots and bolt-holes for a wooden door were also discovered.

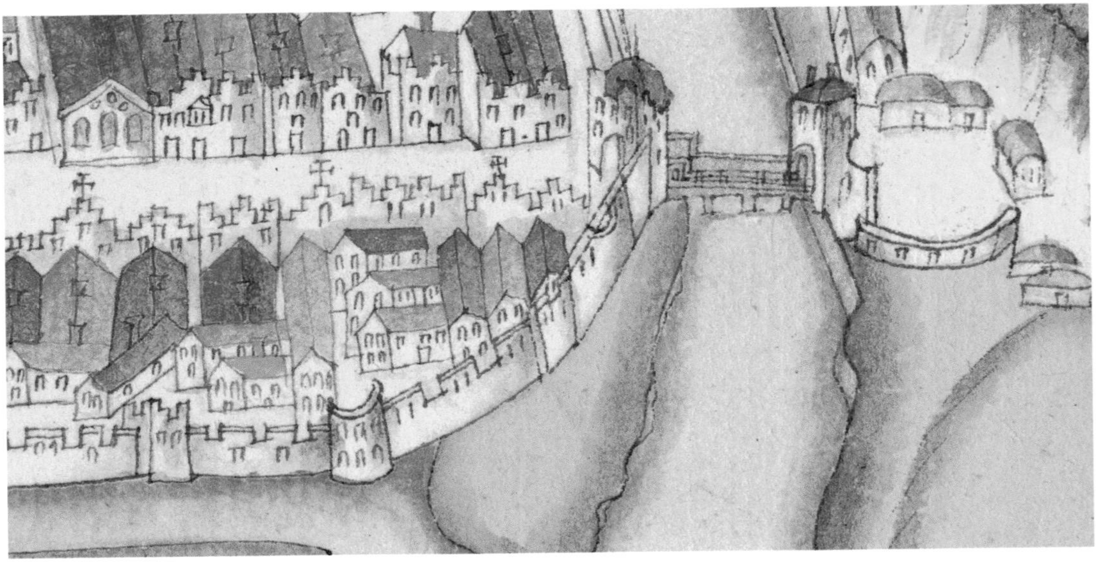

Sketch of the north-east town wall, North Main Street, from George Carew's Map of Cork, *c.* 1601. (Courtesy of Cork City Library)

At the north-west end of the excavation the foundations of a tower or mural turret were found. This was one of the towers that were located regularly along the circuit of the town wall. The tower had a strong base faced with dressed limestone blocks on the battered foundation. It had a shaped projection from the town wall.

The archaeological report concludes that the town wall, which would have functioned as a quay as well as a defensive wall, may have stood to a height of 6 metres or more. Over the course of the 500 years that it was in use, up to 3 metres of silt and debris from human occupation amassed on either side of it. When it was razed to ground level in the eighteenth century the lower wall levels remained, sealed below the ground.

Many artefacts were found. Nearly 10,000 pottery sherds were unearthed, with many of them hailing from wine jugs imported from the Saintonge area of south-west France and from Bristol, England. Many artefacts made from wood, leather and bone were also uncovered.

There were 10 metres of town wall that were preserved for public display purposes underneath the entrance ramp into Kyrl's Quay multistorey car park. The current key holder is the Cork City Council Executive Archaeologist.

In addition, the archaeological report pertaining to the Kyrl's Quay redevelopment (published by Cork Corporation and edited by archaeologist Maurice Hurley) is a worthy addition to the library of any urban scholar.

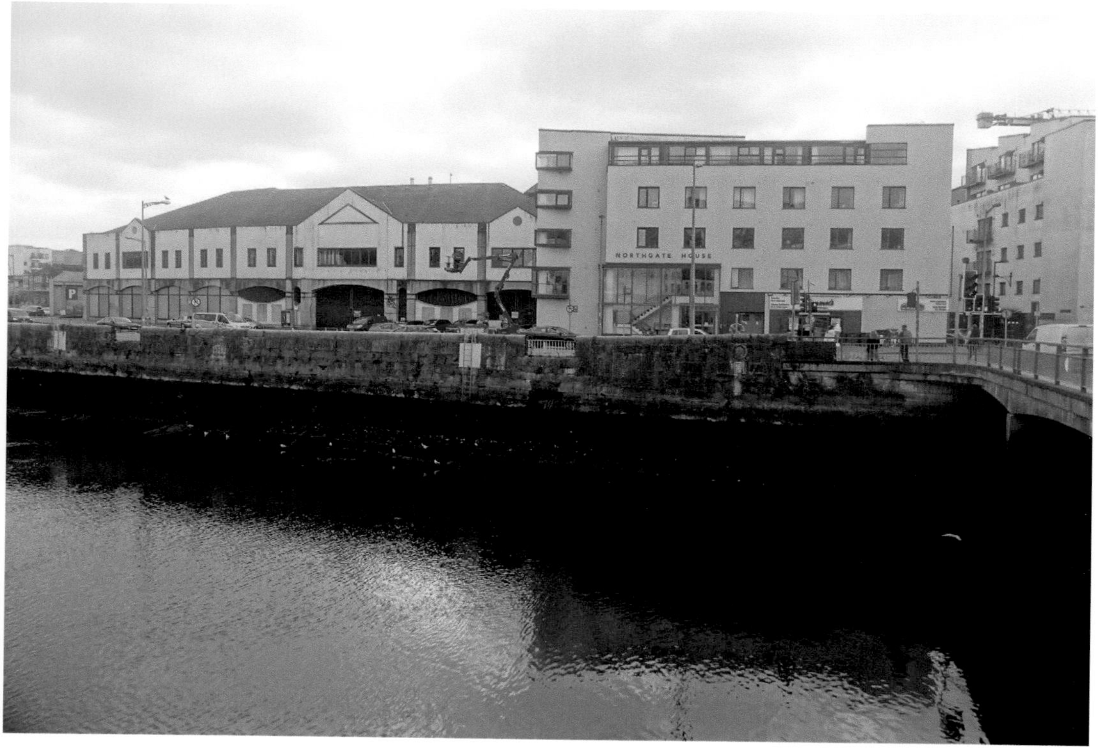

Kyrl's Quay.

26

The 1853 Flood and North Gate Bridge

As the northern access route into the walled town, North Gate drawbridge was a wooden structure annually subjected to severe winter flooding, being almost destroyed in each instance. In May 1711, agreement was reached by members of Cork Corporation of the City that North Gate Bridge be rebuilt in stone in 1712, while in 1713 South Gate Bridge would be replaced with arched stone structures.

In the opening week of November 1853, North Gate Bridge became responsible for large portions of the city being destroyed due to the high floodwaters. *The London Illustrated News* documented the event on 12 November 1853. The rains of Monday and Tuesday of that fateful week amounted to a total of 2½ inches. However, 5 inches had fallen in the preceding fortnight. This, coupled with a new moon, a rising tide of just over 20 feet and hurricane conditions blowing from the south-east caused the elevation of the water levels in the city's channels.

As a result, on the Tuesday evening water started to rise at 4 p.m., and in the space of just thirty minutes the entire flat of the city was inundated. Every moment the water continued rising, higher and higher until the turn of the tide at 5 p.m.

Even though by 8 p.m. the tide had been on the ebb for three hours, the rush of water from Sunday's Well began to rapidly increase. Water tore down the channel in torrid waves inundating the Western Road and the Mardyke, which were speedily impassable. Baths on the Western Road are noted as being carried away by a torrent.

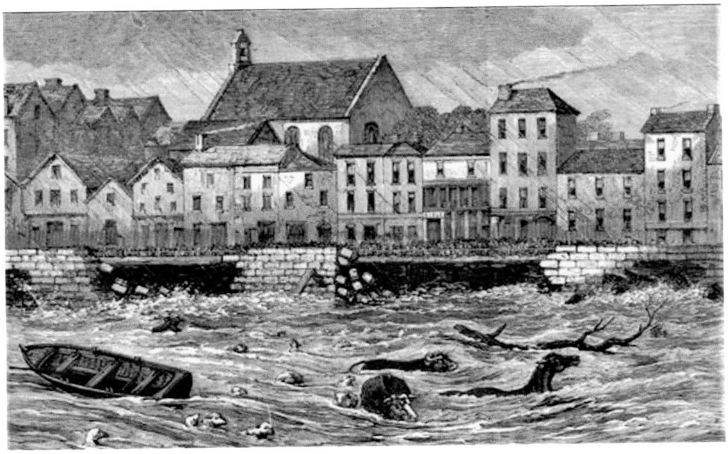

Illustration of the 1853 flood at North Gate Bridge from the *Illustrated London News*. (Courtesy of Cork City Library)

Soon after 10 p.m. the rush of water at North Gate Bridge – the arches of which were very narrow – became so great that the torrent speedily overflowed its banks and bore down Great George's Street (now Washington Street) like a river. The lower parts of the Grand Parade, George's Street, St Patrick's Street and all the streets and lanes in the vicinity were inundated. By 11 p.m. these streets, as well as North Main Street and South Main Street, were filled with water several feet deep.

Halfway down Lavitt's Quay was a fountain, at the immediate edge of the river. Suddenly, a loud crash was heard, and the fountain had disappeared and around 30 feet of the quay wall had been carried away. The water, having secured another access point, rushed rapidly over the quay, overwhelming the houses. Seconds later, another portion of quay wall was torn down. On the opposite side of the river, a portion of the sewer burst and part of the quay fell in.

At 12.30 a.m., the flood, far from diminishing, was acquiring additional fury. The waters were dashing under the arches of St Patrick's Bridge carrying chairs, beams of timber, trees, etc. Suddenly a terrible crash was heard, followed by a piercing shriek. A great piece of the bridge had given way, taking with it eleven people. They were borne down with the tide and all drowned, except for one who was rescued.

Barriers of timber were immediately put into place and police and a party of military people were soon in attendance to warn folks not to cross it. A few moments later another large mass of masonry gave way and was carried into the tide.

In June 1856, an Act was passed to enable the mayor, alderman and burgesses of Cork to remove certain bridges and build new ones. Subsequently, a new North Gate Bridge and St Patrick's Bridge were reconstructed.

The foundation stone for the fourth-known North Gate Bridge was laid in April 1863. The new bridge was to be a cast-iron structure with the ironwork completed by Ranking & Co. of Liverpool. Nearly 100 years later, in 1961, the bridge would have to be reconstructed again due to increased road traffic and heavier vehicles.

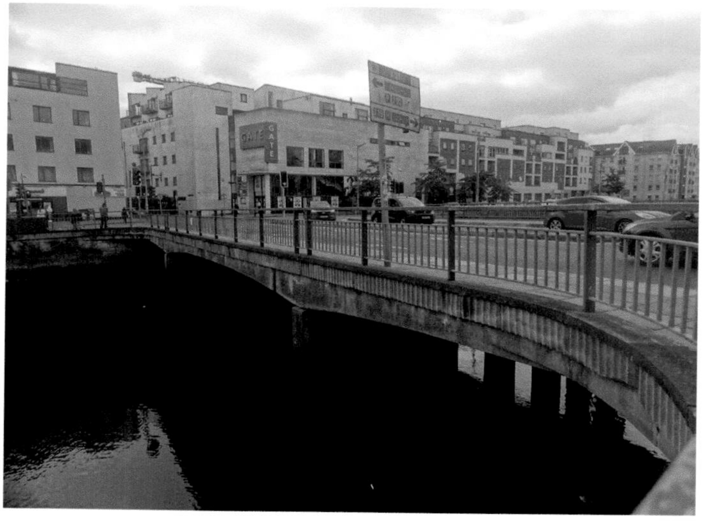

North Gate Bridge today.

A Taste of Tanora – The 1779 Arch

Hidden behind North Gate Bridge apartments is an elegant archway with a date of 1779 inscribed on it. The archway was part of John Daly & Co. Mineral Water Manufacturers. The style suggests a late nineteenth-century, Victorian date. The 1779 archway was once part of the entrance door to the offices, one of Cork's oldest firms reputedly established in 1779, located on Kyrl's Quay. This was a well-established, presumably wealthy firm (later having owned the Victoria Hotel and Bonded Warehouses on Kyrl's Quay). The status of the company and the style of the arch suggests that it was made for the Daly offices on Kyrl's Quay.

In 1915, John Daly and Co. were also the original creators of the well-known Tanora brand – a tangerine-flavoured drink. At that time, temperance groups lobbied manufacturers of lemonade such as John Daly's to produce another popular non-alcoholic drink. Tanora was created through the importation of tangerine oranges.

Fifty years ago, Daly's owned Kyrl's Quay Bonded Warehouses and the Victoria Hotel in Cork. Daly's also bought the total issued share capital of Coca-Cola Bottling (Dublin). They had the Coca-Cola franchise for Munster, which gave Daly's extensive interests in the Irish market for soft drinks. However, it was a Munster Coca-Cola bottling company that eventually bought out the company.

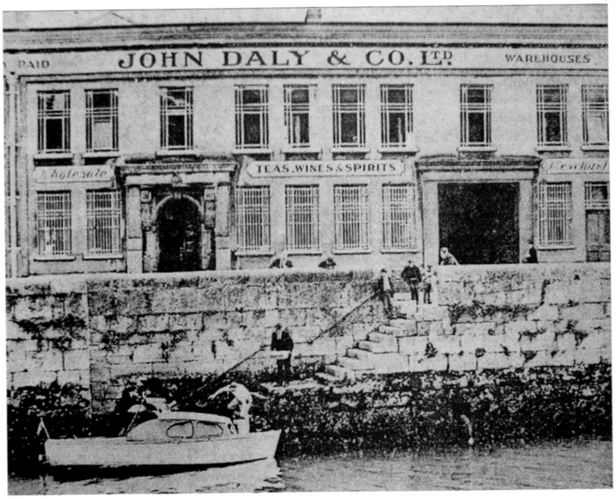

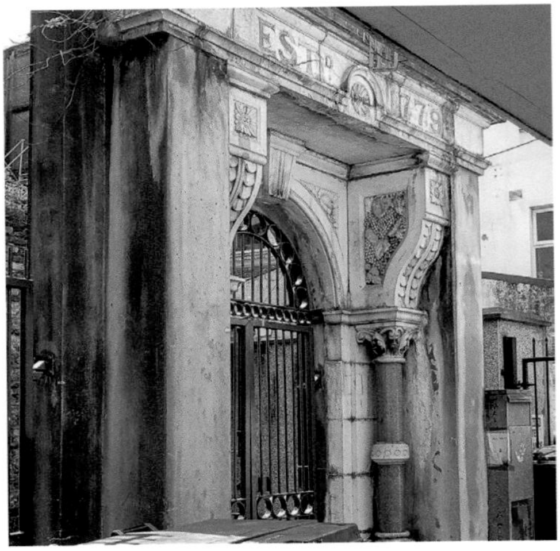

Above left: John Daly & Co. warehouses, Kyrl's Quay, 1970s. (Courtesy of Cork City Library)

Above right: Historical archway (1779) now embedded behind buildings off Kyrl's Quay.

28

In Context, Shandon Street

Shandon Street is strategically aligned to follow a large indentation across a sandstone ridge on Cork's north side. It harnesses the indentation to great effect. Today the street has a mix of architecture from the late eighteenth and nineteenth centuries. Shandon Street was part of the Wide Street Commission's project in the 1820s.

One can envisage that the route may have possibly begun its life as a muddy trackway leading down to the river from a ringfort called Sean Dún, or in English 'old fort'. Certainly, the area was strategic enough in Anglo-Norman times for the colonialists to seize the ringfort and built a castle on it. The said castle was manned by the Prendergast, then the de Cogans and then the Barry family.

On early seventeenth-century maps the castle is shown as having exterior laneways, such as the existing Dominick Street, which connected to Shandon Street. Such maps also show a handful of houses, but how representative these are of real population figures is unknown.

Another important marker was St Mary's Church, which was built sometime in the Middle Ages. In 1536, its rector, Dominick Terry, was made the first Protestant Bishop of Cork. This first church was destroyed during the Siege of Cork and rebuilt in the guise of St Ann's Church on the site. It is unsure why the name change occurred. A second

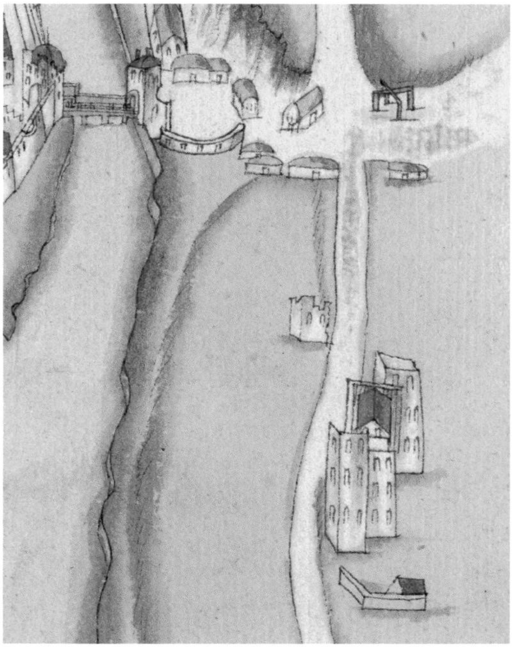

Sketch of Shandon Castle, North Main Street from George Carew's Map of Cork, *c.* 1601. (Courtesy of Cork City Library)

St Mary's Church was created, though, and this stood near the foot of Shandon Street (east side). It was taken down in 1879 and a third church was consecrated in 1879 by Bishop John Gregg, which is situated at Sunday's Well.

In post-medieval Cork the first recorded church on the site of St Mary's and St Anne's North Cathedral is from 1624, which in itself would have attracted a settlement of housing around it. Certainly, by Carty's Map of 1726 a distinctive Chapel Lane is marked on the map, which runs from the adjacent River Kiln Valley. The eighteenth century also coincided with the creation of Skiddy's Almshouse and the North Infirmary east of St Anne's. By John Rocque's map of 1750, butter market buildings are shown adjacent the latter buildings.

Meanwhile, on the western side of Shandon, Fair Hill gave access to thousands of cattle to local slaughter houses. In addition, eighteenth- and early nineteenth-century maps show the progressive growth of laneways, which by the early twentieth century were over 20 acres in size and now some of the worse slums in the city – they were only demolished in the early 1930s.

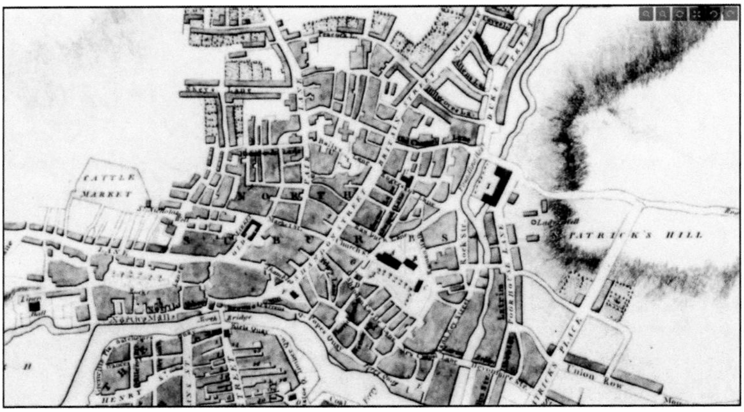

Section of Beaufort's Map of Cork (1801) showing Shandon Street and its various laneways and butter market (buildings are marked A, B and C). (Courtesy of Cork City Library)

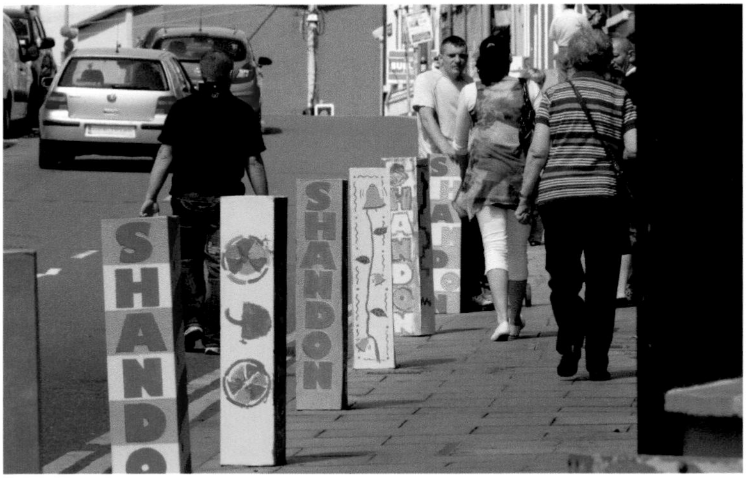

Celebrating Shandon Street.

29

Shandon Castle

The Firkin Crane Dance Cork centre now marks the site of the original ringfort of Sean Dún or Old Fort. George Carew's *c.* 1600 map of Cork places an emphasis on a two-towered structure called Shandon Castle, which replaced the old ringfort. From aligning old maps with newer ones of the city, we can establish that the castle was on the site of what is now the Firkin Crane.

Between 1599 and 1600, George Carew, Lord President of Munster, having undertaken his suppression of rebellion, took up his quarters at Shandon Castle overlooking the walled town of Cork and its adjacent hinterland. It was a building of great physical and symbolic strength. Courts for criminal cases were frequently held here by the Lord President and the judge on circuit. Those who rose up against the Munster Plantation were likewise imprisoned there.

Urban myth pitches Shandon Castle as standing on the verge of a precipice overhanging the Lee. It has been depicted as a kind of medieval castle keep with a large portcullis gate. Steep stairs called the Giant's Steps leading to the nearby River Lee were cut through this precipice.

An article by Revd James Dwyer in the *Journal of the Cork Historical and Archaeological Society* in 1897 notes that the steps were removed in the 1860s (possibly to create the

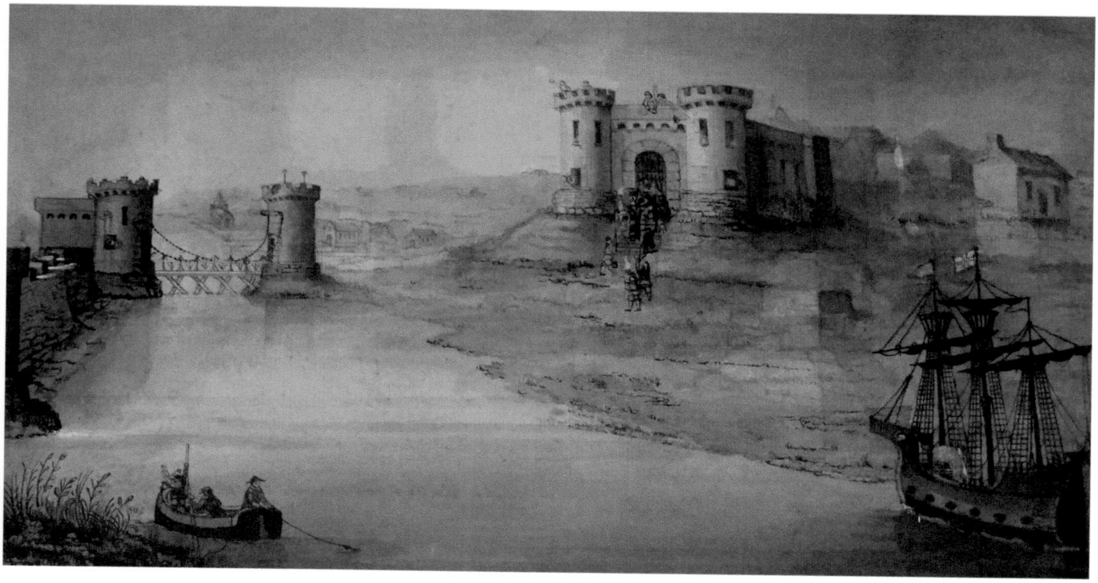

Depiction of Shandon Castle, *c.* 1603. (Courtesy of Cork City Museum)

laneways that now exist in the area, such as Rowland's Lane and surrounds). The street adjoining the castle was popularly known by the name of 'Shandon Castle Lane, which is now Dominick Street.

The castle is originally said to have been built by the Prendergasts. It passed to the de Cogans and the Barrys and served as a manorial feudal centre until Carew's arrival.

Woulfe's *Irish Names and Surnames* (1923) highlights that the Barry surname occurs in the earliest Anglo-Irish records and has always been associated with the County of Cork. In 1179, Robert FitzStephen granted to his nephew Philip de Barry the three cantreds of Ui Liatháin, Muscraighe-trí-máighe and Cinel Aodha, represented in time by the baronies of Barrymore, Orrery, and Kinalea. This grant was confirmed by King John in 1207 to William de Barry, son and heir of Philip.

30

Interior Glories at St Anne's Church, Shandon

St Anne's, Shandon, was built in 1722 to replace the older and local church of St Mary's, Shandon, which was destroyed in the Siege of Cork in 1690 by English forces. In 1750 the firm of Abel Rudhall in Gloucester cast the famous bells of Shandon. On 7 December 1752, the bells were first used and were rung in celebration and recognition of the marriage of a certain Mr Henry Harding to Miss Catherine Dorman. Inscriptions can be found on the bells, which contain messages of joy and death.

The architecture of the church and tower is an Early English style. The peculiar feature of the tall church tower (approximately 40 metres heigh) is that the north and east sides are comprised of red sandstone while the south and west sides are composed of grey hewn limestone.

Significant alterations in changes in the interior furnishings have been made from time to time. An upper gallery was removed, the side galleries were removed and the monuments were lowered to the position they are in today. The box pews were replaced by traditional pews and the former plaster ceiling was replaced by a timber barrel-vaulted ceiling.

Two relics from the medieval St Mary's Church survive in St Anne's Church. The font, which is still in use by the parish to this day, bears the inscription: 'Walter Elinton, William Ring 1629 Made this Pant at their charges.' The Piercy Memorial is to be seen fixed on the wall of the vestry room. It marked the burial place in the old church of George Piercy, Esq., who died in 1635.

The east window, portraying the Transfiguration of Our Lord is of remarkable beauty; the window is a memorial to the family of Lotamore and was presented by George Abraham Wood in 1883. It was attributed to Mayer & Co., Munich. Another window, showing the Parable of the Good Samaritan, was erected in 1882 by Clement Dunscombe in memory of Nicholas Dunscombe.

The small oculus-style memorial window of St Luke Healing, which is near the nave of the church with vivid colours and realistic treatment, is a striking example of modern stained-glass work. It was erected in 1937 as a tribute to Dr Philip Lee, a much beloved physician and devoted churchman. The window is attributed to artist Hubert McGoldrick of the co-operative studio An Túr Gloine based in Dublin from 1903 to 1944.

A number of past worshippers are commemorated by mural tablets. Worthy of note are those commemorating Revd George Barton, curate of the parish, who died in 1832, a victim of his charity work during the spread of cholera.

The 1914–18 war memorial is a very fine example of its type, and was designed by Richard Caulfield Orpen of Dublin. It comprises three marble panels. The centre panel has a mosaic of St George in full armour, holding a lance bearing his banner, and a drawn sword. The side panels have gilded edges and bear the names of the fallen. The panels are framed in marble pillars with a canopy.

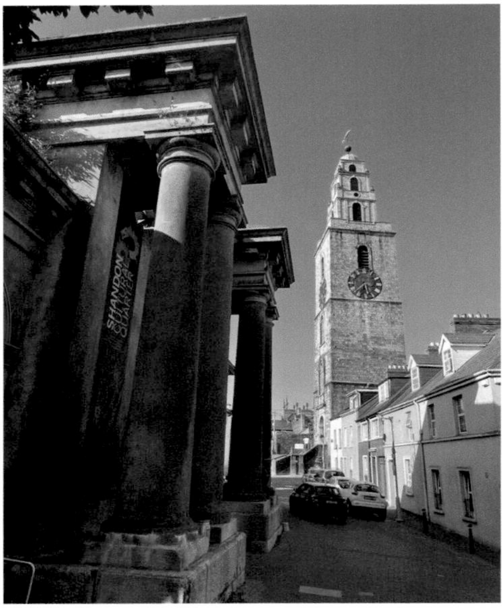

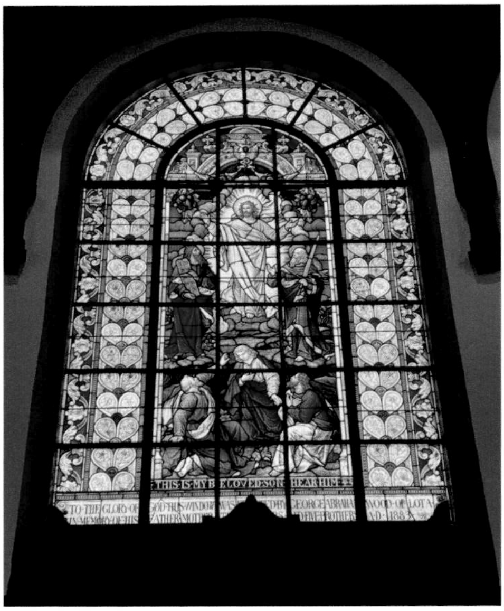

Above left: Exterior view of the tower of St Anne's Church, Shandon.

Above right: The east window, portraying the Transfiguration of Our Lord, is attributed to Mayer & Co., Munich.

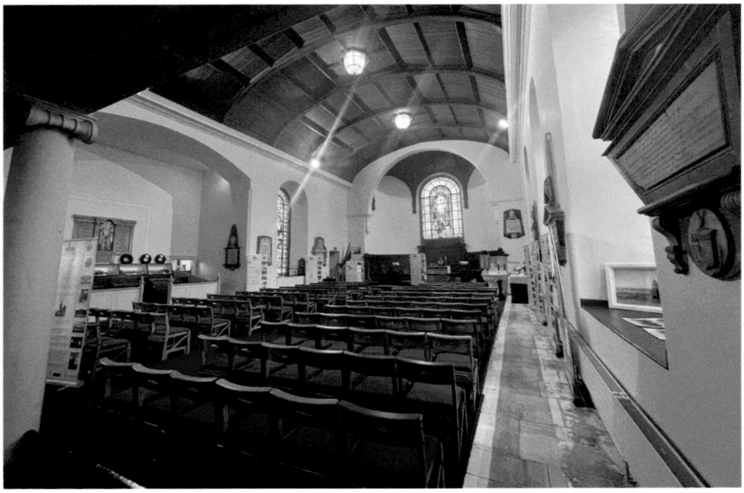

Interior view of St Anne's Church, Shandon.

31

The North Infirmary

Just east of Shandon Street, the foundation stone of North Infirmary Hospital was laid on 25 December 1720. Several months later, the building was completed and contained three floors with four rooms on each.

In the 1840s the infirmary was rebuilt and considerably enlarged. Initially it contained twenty-eight beds; the rebuilding made space for 110 beds. In 1842, there were 558 patients admitted, and 17,630 attended as externs. It was attended by two physicians and two surgeons. Its total income, derived from subscriptions, Parliamentary and Grand Jury grants, was £1,100 3*s* 1*d*, out of which £205 14*s* 11*d* was paid in salaries.

An extensive annual report of the activities of the North Infirmary appears in the *Cork Examiner* on 6 May 1919, which provides insights into staff, public demand, hospital space and financial debt. The City High Sheriff Mr W. J. O'Sullivan, subsequently the Lord Mayor, presided. The infirmary opened the year's work with sixty-eight beds occupied by intern patients, which consisted of fifty-seven surgical and eleven medical cases. There were 1,054 surgical and 291 medical patients received during the year. Of this large number, 1,033 patients were discharged, cured or relieved, and 252 of the latter were positively treated.

During May 1918 to May 1919, there were deaths of thirty-five surgical and thirty medical patients. A large number of patients from distant parts of the county were treated by the surgeon. As an addition to the main building (opened in 1836 with its wings opening in 1893), a new dental hospital had been opened. In another portion of the new building patients were treated for diseases of the eye, ear, throat and nose. This department, under Dr J. H. Horgan, was deemed much sought after. Owing to the war and other causes, the Rontgen Ray Department had not yet been formally opened, although it was being used for some infirmary purposes.

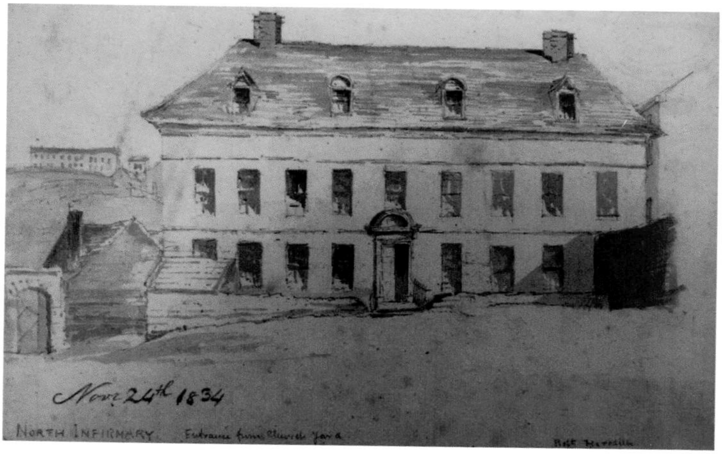

North Infirmary, 1834. (Courtesy of Cork Public Museum)

Reference in the annual report is made to the resignation of Mother Josephine Murphy due to sickness. For many years she was the superioress of the Sisters of Charity of St Vincent de Paul, who had charge of the patients and the domestic working of the North Infirmary. Superioress Mother Angela McNally was appointed to the role. There were fourteen sisters in the various wards. Joining them were two staff nurses and a large number of probationers from Cork's nursing school.

The sub-section of the report on the Eye, Throat, Nose and Ear Department described that, with the exception of the period that the influenza epidemic was prevalent in the city, the Ophthalmic and Laryngological Department of the Hospital continued to be largely used by the poor of the city and county during the previous year. Many children also attended the department. This report showed that parents of impoverished children were beginning to realise that the early and expert treatment of defects of the eyes, ears and breathing passages was the 'best and only safeguard against the permanent injury of the organs'. Over 2,000 new cases visited the extern division of this department during the year, and the total attendances were nearly three times that number. Nearly 300 surgical operations – many of a serious character – were performed under general anaesthesia, and approximately 150 operations were performed under local anaesthesia.

The infirmary's history is peppered with tales of hardship and examples of perseverance to maintain a place of care for the sick in the impoverished northside of Cork during the 1700s and 1800s. The battles to fend off threats of closure were faced and won. Crises were overcome because the management committees could depend on voluntary funding. Indeed, the hospital flourished and expanded, thanks to the pennies of the people of Cork.

However, in 1987, due to national health cuts, the hospital closed, resulting in 205 redundancies. Despite vocal and physical protests from far and wide, there was to be no last-minute reprieve. The doors were finally closed on 27 November 1987. Ten years later the building's next host was the Shandon Court Hotel (now the Maldron Hotel).

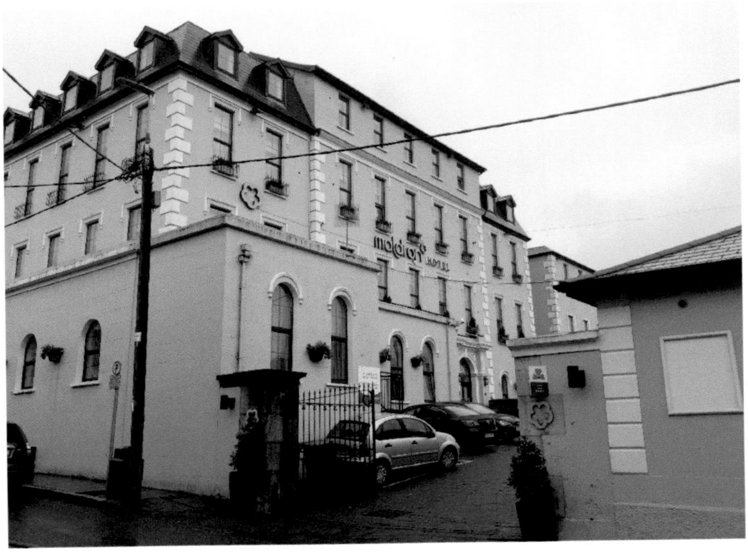

Maldron Hotel, former site of North Infirmary, Cork.

32

The North Cathedral

The present Cathedral of St Mary and St Anne is the fifth church on the site since the early seventeenth century (1624, 1700, 1730, 1808 and 1828 with mid- to late nineteenth-century additions).

On 4 June 1787, a new bishop arrived by the name of Francis Moylan. His ambition was to assist the spiritual demands of the diocese by building a cathedral. Its construction began in 1799 and was completed nine years later in August 1808. On Monday 22 August 1808, the new North Cathedral was devoted to the Blessed Virgin Mary and St Anne. It was one of the earliest examples of neo-Gothic style in the city. The chapel was in a cruciform shape with side aisles, a nave and transepts.

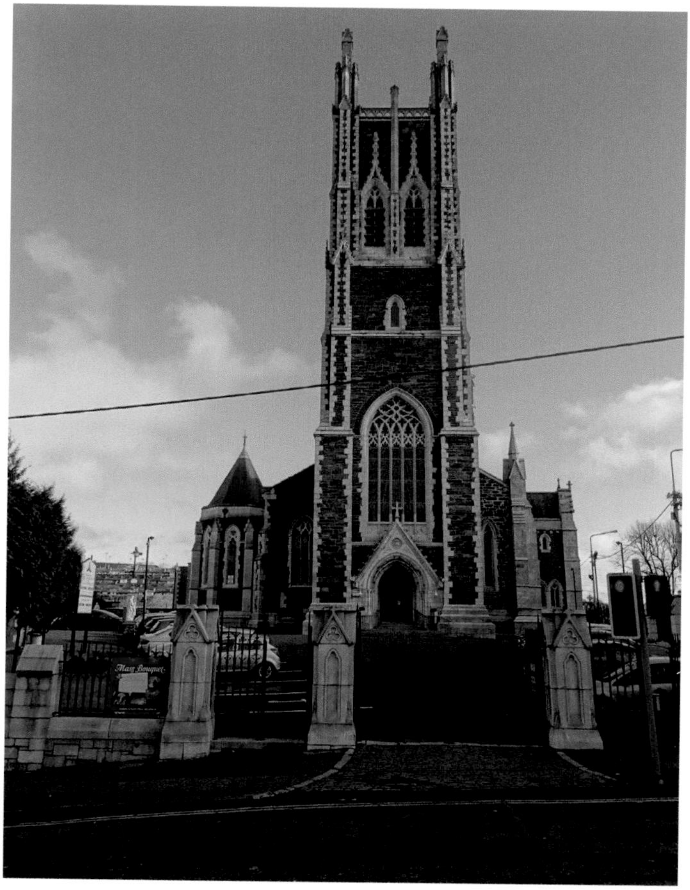

Exterior view of North Cathedral.

In 1820, an immense fire greatly damaged the cathedral so much so that it was really just the skeleton structure of the burned cathedral that survived. However, all was not lost. Shortly after, the bishop of that time, John Murphy, delegated the architect Mr George R. Pain to the rebuilding of the twelve-year-old cathedral. George is also responsible for buildings such as Holy Trinity, St Patrick's Church and Blackrock Castle.

Around 1828, George Pain's renovation of the church began. He first disposed of the side aisles and substituted them with a large gallery at the western end – today it is only used by the choir. The Gothic style of architecture was used again, this time to emphasise the nameless saints on the roof. Arches could again be seen, but this time a very small crevice was to be observed in the middle of the design. These arches were high up and could be described as clerestory windows or blind arcading today.

The main altar was the next task to be accomplished. Mr John Hogan, an apprentice of Sir Thomas Deane, another famous architect of the time, was chosen to redesign the altar – Deane had recommended him to Bishop Murphy. Hogan positioned twenty-seven statues at intervals around the altar. The cathedra was of carved oak, as was the pulpit. Again, sculptured angels were placed over both structures.

Between 1862 and 1867 Canon Daniel Foley's Tower was worked on. Unfortunately, though, the project was a complete disaster as there were virtually no funds for the tower. As such, Canon Foley became the builder, stonemason, etc. The architect was Sir John Benson.

By mid-July in 1869, most of the outer features were completed, including the parapets, spire and turrets-minarets. The bells of the church were placed in position in 1870. Another feature of the newly constructed cathedral was the great western door, which can still be seen today. It is inspired from fourteenth-century designs and its top takes the form of a pointed arch.

In 1964, the cathedral was extended in length again and various new rooms were added, such as a new sacristy and rooms for parish groups. Today the layout of the cathedral remains the same; however in 1996 a major refurbishment took place of the interior while, on the outside, the roof was replaced and the walls cleaned and renovated.

33

Chapel Lane and the First North Monastery

In the late nineteenth century, just a third of local poor children aged between five and fourteen attended school. One-third of the poor population were unable to read or write. For the poorer classes, there were several free public schools in the early nineteenth century.

In 1802, in Waterford, a new religious congregation was founded named the Society of the Presentation under the auspices of Edmund Rice. The Bishop of Cork, Francis Moylan, wished to establish a branch in Cork. In 1811, that wish was fulfilled, and the already existing Cork Charitable North School was taken over by the Presentation Brothers on the northside of the city. Such was the success of the order in treating some of the miseries of the poor children in Cork, further schools were built in the city.

The North Monastery School was founded on 9 November 1811 when two Christian brothers, Brother Jerome O'Connor and Brother John Baptist Leonard, were given charge of a school in Chapel Lane by the North Cathedral by the Bishop of Cork, Revd Dr Moylan. Seventeen students attended on the first day.

In 1814 a 14-acre sloping site was acquired from a wealthy Roman Catholic businessman, Sir George Gould, and a new school was built. The North Monastery had found its permanent home. The historic building still stands complete with two modern-day school buildings in the immediate vicinity.

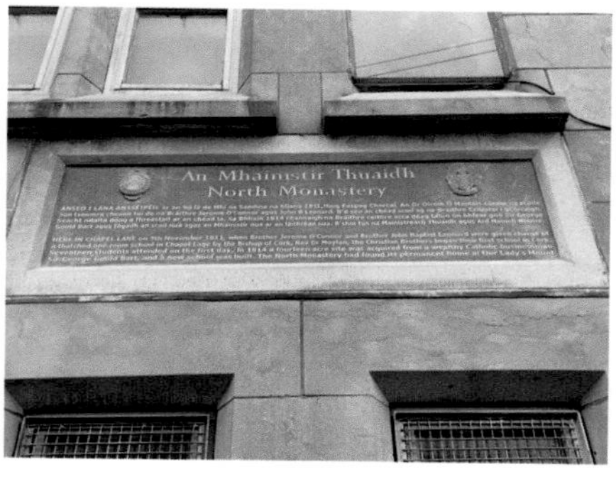

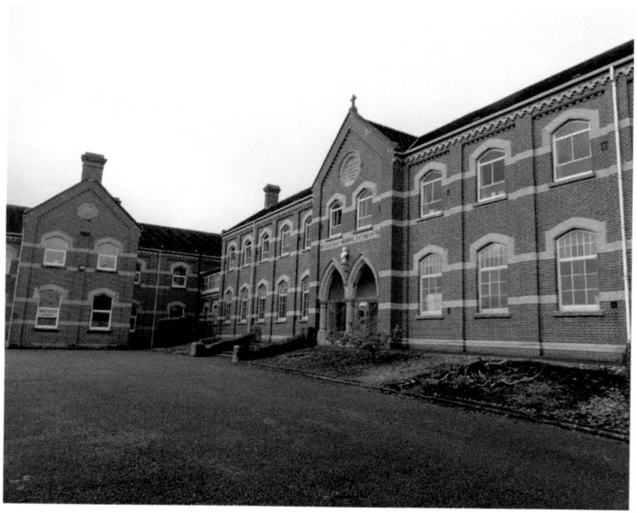

Above: Memorial plaque at North Cathedral remembering the original North Monastery School.

Right: North Monastery School Memorial Extension, built 1911.

34

Gurranabraher and the Irish Free State City

Cork in the 1920s and 1930s could be described as a city rising from the ashes. The arson attack by the Black and Tans during the Irish War of Independence (11 December 1920) on St Patrick Street, Cork City Hall and the Carnegie Library remained as scars on the physical landscape of the city well into the 1930s. Their slow rebuild resulted in a myriad of debates (and even rows) by the city's business community and the Corporation on how best to rebuild these municipal landscapes.

The dissolution of the elected members of the Corporation in 1924 (due to corruption charges) led central government to appoint Philip Monahan as city commissioner. He was appointed in November 1924. In the early 1920s he had been mayor of Drogheda and a member of Louth County Council. Concurrently, he was also a commissioner in Kerry by the age of twenty-six. Finding his feet quickly in Cork, by March 1925 he was talking to the press and setting out his goals.

Using some of Westminster's compensation package for the burning of parts of the city, he sidelined the rebuilding of City Hall and set about acquiring new designs. He set aside £25,000 for the installation of a new filtration plant at the waterworks, invested £50,000 for the asphalting of 68,000 square yards of streets, pushed for the completion

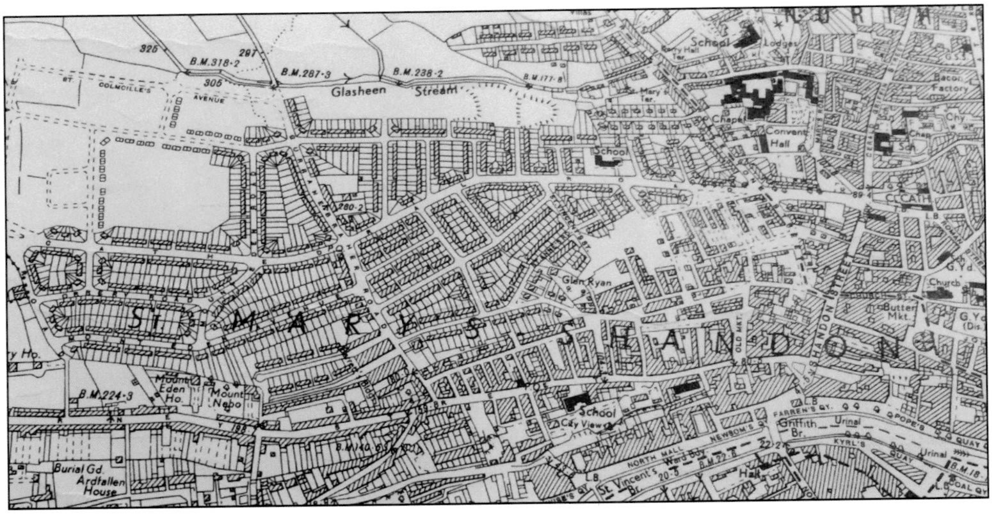

Map of Gurranabraher, *c.* 1935. (Courtesy of Cork City Library)

of the rebuilding of St Patrick's Street, the rebuilding of Parnell Bridge, the purification of the city's sewage schemes, the replacement of the eighteenth-century culverts under St Patrick's Street with new sewers, strove to create a new cattle market for the city and took over of management of what the press called the 'Mental Hospital' in Sunday's Well (now the site of Our Lady's Hospital).

The founding of the Cork Town Planning Association in 1922 marked the beginning of a serious attempt to deal with the problem of the dreadful housing conditions in parts of the Middle Parish and the areas around Barrack Street, Shandon Street and Blarney Street.

In 1926 Philip Monahan called for the adoption of 'Cork: A Civic Survey', which recognised the need for the clearance of the slums in the city.

As early as March 1925, Monahan invested £70,000 for the provision of 200 houses in Turners Cross. He also put down his marker that he was to ensure efficiency in the local public sector. He pursued an agenda to reduce the wage of Corporation workers to 4*s* 6*d* per week by the threat of using direct labour. A total of 468 social housing units were constructed in Turners Cross between 1926 and 1932.

Somewhere around November 1932, the first plans were completed for 250 social housing houses in Gurranabraher, and the first steps were taken towards their erection. A two-page spread in the *Cork Examiner* on 19 March 1934 (pages 6–7) describes that the project gave work to some 300 labourers. The architect for the scheme was Mr J. R. Boyd Barrett, South Mall, and the building was entrusted to two firms, Messrs Murray and Lane and Mr E. Barrett. Over 300,000 red roof tiles were supplied by the Cork Tile Co. (Messrs W. J. Hickey and Co., Maylor Street).

Eleven saints were honoured in the housing scheme, namely St Mary, St Bridget, St Ann, St Philomena, St Theresa, St Rita, St Declan, St Vincent, St Enda, St Colmcille and St Anthony.

Most significantly for the tenants, the amount of rent due was to be governed by the amount of each tenant's income.

From the mid-1930s onwards, further housing units were planned and began to be constructed in Fair Hill and Greenmount. The development of land in Ballyphehane also began but was hampered by the advent of the Second World War.

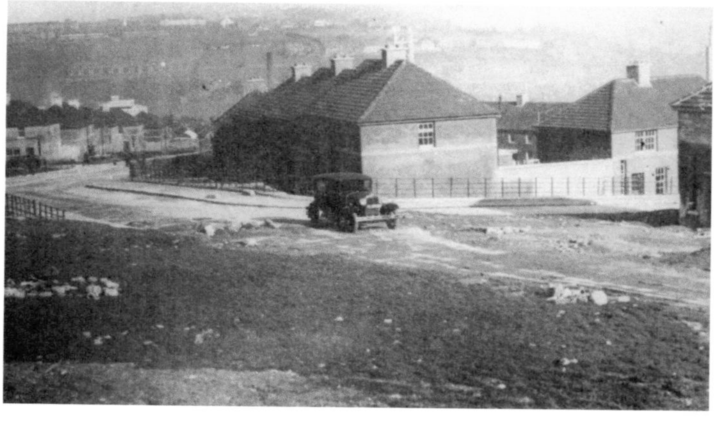

Gurranabraher, 17 March 1934. (Courtesy of *Irish Examiner* Archives)

35

Patriotism and Gerald Griffin Street

Gerald Griffin Street was formerly called Mallow Lane. In 1832, Mallow Lane was renamed Clarence Street after the Duke of Clarence, who was an outspoken advocate of Catholic emancipation.

Born in Limerick, Gerald Griffin (1803–40) was a poet, playwright and Irish novelist. In 1823, he emigrated to London and got a job as a reporter for one of the daily papers. He later turned to writing fiction. One of his most famous works is *The Irish Collegians*, which was written about the murder of the Colleen Bawn in 1820.

In 1838 Gerald joined the Christian Brothers at the North Monastery and burned all of his unpublished manuscripts. He died from typhus fever at the age of thirty-six.

In November 1898, the motion of Cllr John O'Neil of Cork Corporation was accepted to change the name of Clarence Street to Gerald Griffin Street. Gerald Griffin has a street named after him in Limerick City and another in Cork City, Ireland. Loughill/Ballyhahill GAA club in west Limerick play under the name of Gerald Griffins.

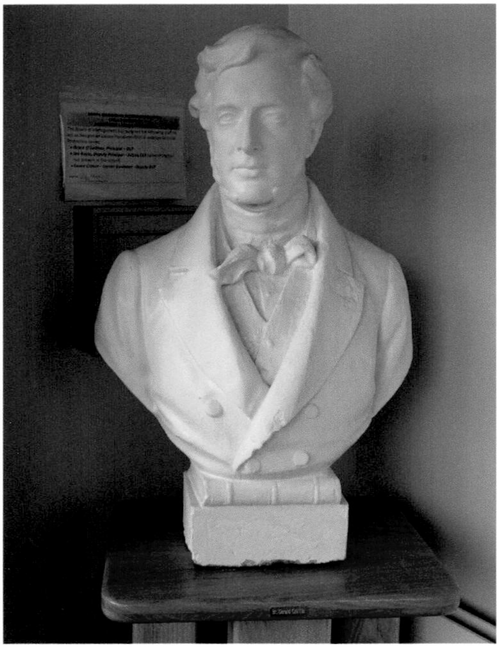

Bust of Gerald Griffin located in North Monastery Secondary School.

Presentation Sisters Convent Site

The Presentation Sisters Convent Complex is striking on Gerald Griffin Street. Nano Nagle opened her first school in 1754 with around thirty students. It was on Cove Lane, on what is now the site of Nano Nagle Place on Douglas Street. She was a great educator and believed education was the key to a better life for people. Within nine months she was educating 200 girls, and by 1757 she had opened seven schools – five for girls and two for boys.

Nano Nagle (1718–84) set up three small hovel schools in the North Parish. The first was in Philpott-Curran Lane at the back of the cathedral presbytery and was the school for girls. The others were at the end of Shandon Street and strictly for boys. One was located on the left-hand side, at the very end of Shandon Street, an attic at the top of a four-storey house, while the other was on the little lane running at the side of where O'Connor's Funeral Home now stands at the North Gate Bridge.

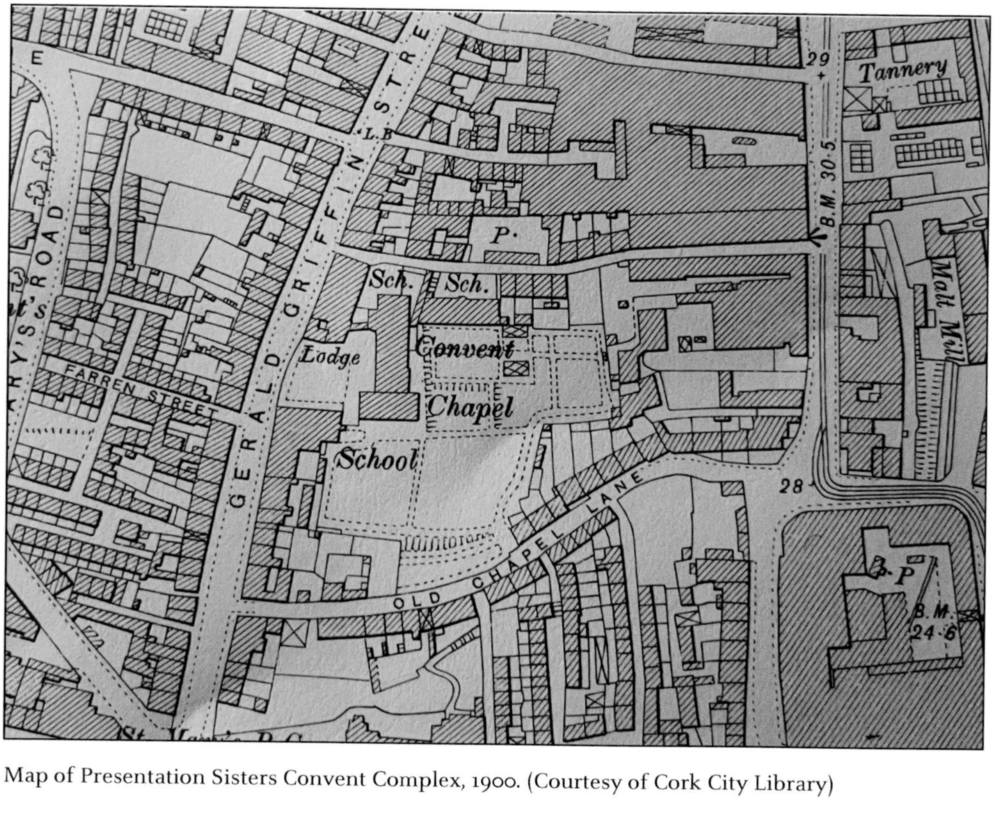

Map of Presentation Sisters Convent Complex, 1900. (Courtesy of Cork City Library)

It was in the year 1799 that the Presentation Sisters came to live in the North Parish. Bishop Moylan sent four ladies to South Presentation for training, and after taking their vows they returned to a Philpott Curran Lane. A local lady, Barbara Goold, had a second storey added onto her house and the sisters lived there while teaching hundreds of children until 15 January 1813.

The sisters needed a convent and a school and Bishop Moylan asked local priest Fr John England to take on the project. It took a long time to find enough money to buy a site; they eventually purchased a site at Hill Grove Lane from the Tanning Yard.

The infant school was replaced in 1871 through a plan to enlarge the schoolrooms and facilities. It was formerly opened on 16 January 1872. It was designed by Sir John Benson and built by Edmund and Peter O'Flynn. It is now disused. A modern Presentation School stands nearby.

As well as a school, a presentation convent and chapel were built. The chapel, which is said to date between 1820 and 1830, is thought to be the work of Presentation Brother and architect Revd Michael Augustine Riordan, who was also involved in the Ursuline Convent in Blackrock. To the north is the four-storey convent building, built *c.* 1830.

The present primary school was built in 1965–67 and the old building was then used as a secondary school until the group moved to Farranree in 1976.

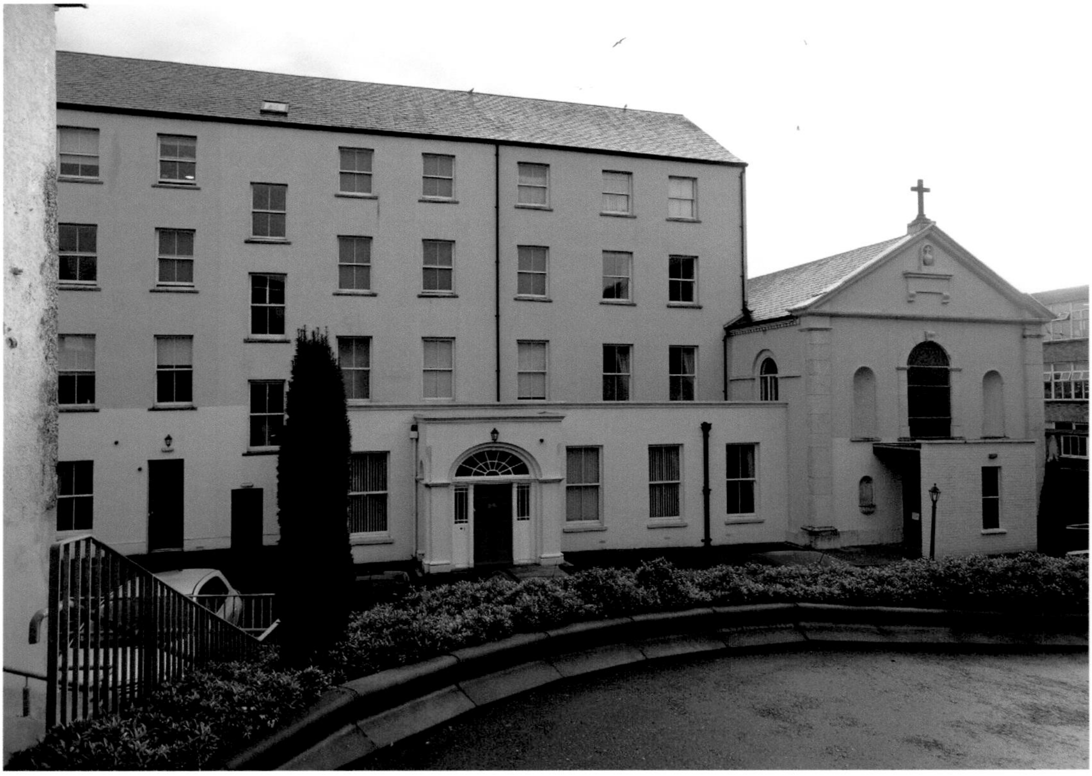

Presentation Sisters Convent Complex.

37

Basketball and Neptune Stadium

Neptune is the second oldest basketball club in Ireland, the oldest being Corinthians of Dublin. Neptune, as the club has become colloquially and popularly known, was founded in *c*. 1947 within the Irish Defence Forces Slua Muirí – hence the nautical name.

On 9 February 1948 hundreds of Cork sporting enthusiasts will witness a treat to which they have long been looking forward: the first public exhibitions of basketball, a game that had made unusual strides both in popularity and style in the city during previous months.

Neptune stadium opened

THE continuing growth of basketball in Ireland, and particularly in Cork, was fully illustrated at yesterday's opening to the public of the new £½ million Neptune Basketball Club stadium, at St. Catherine's Square, off Gerald Griffin Street, in the heart of Cork's northside.

A capacity crowd of over three thousand spectators crammed into the venue for the Burgerland/Jameson International, Dublin, National Cup quarter-final tie, which Burgerland won by 95-93 after five minutes overtime, to knock out the holders.

Burgerland now join Team Britvic, Cork; Team Harp Lager, Cork and Gleneagle Killarney in the National Cup play-offs to be held at the new 3,500-seater stadium over the weekend of January 19-20 next.

There was disappoint-

Irish Basketball Association, Mr. Liam McGinn, a member of the Neptune club, said that the opening of the stadium marked the greatest milestone in the history of the Association, and added that it was the first custom-built basketball arena of its kind in the country.

"This had come after fifteen years of hard graft from the club and from the stadium committee in particular. Since I have become president of the IBBA, I have said many times that the principal impediment to the growth of our sport has been the

Story: Noel Spillane
Camera: Eddie O'Hare

Extract from *Cork Examiner* on 7 February 1985 showcasing the opening of Neptune Stadium. (Courtesy of Cork City Library)

Up to autumn 1947 the game was played only in very limited circles – Army, LDF, Boy Scouts and a few schools in the city. It was comparatively unknown to the general body of sportsmen, but in the autumn a league was started and the organisers were practically inundated with applications to participate. Prominent among the twenty-odd clubs that were affiliated were members of Cork football teams under all three codes, and the league brought into opposition many well-known players of different games who had never hitherto met on any common ground.

Some years later the Neptune members moved out on their own and founded the northside's famous club. With teams in all grades of the sport, in both male and female competitions, it has become one of the top clubs in the country, with many national awards to its credit, as well as local and provincial trophies.

Fast forward to 1983 and Neptune was one of the biggest clubs in the country, with their senior team playing under the Burgerland International banner, won both the League title and the Roy Curtis international club series in 1982. They were also voted 'Club of the Year' by the Irish Basketball Association.

In July 1983, plans for a new stadium covering 22,000 square feet was proposed, with a seating capacity for over 2,500. The cost of the project was to be met by the club's fundraising activities, including the sale of three-year tickets and advertising space within the stadium.

The new stadium was to be built on a site at St Catherine's Square, which was at the junction of Gerald Griffin Street and Burke's Avenue. The stadium was opened on 1 January 1985 overseen by an attendance of the biggest ever crowd at a basketball game in Ireland and was well in excess of the 2,000 plus crowd.

38

Madden's Buildings

The Artisans and Labourers Dwellings Improvements Acts of 1875 and the Housing of the Working Classes Act of 1890 detailed the importance of eradicating tenement or slum housing. At this time no significant financial aid was available to carry out large-scale clearance. However, Cork Corporation did make an effort. In 1886, new houses were built in Blackpool on the site of an old cattle market. A total of seventy-six houses were planned and built comprising a kitchen, front living room and two overhead bedrooms. The contractor was Edward Fitzgerald and by the end of 1886 they were ready for occupation.

Named the Madden's Buildings after the mayor of the time, Paul Madden, these new houses were to set the scene for a further three housing schemes before the turn of the 1900s. These comprised of Ryan's Buildings, built in 1888 (sixteen houses), the Horgan's Buildings in 1891 (126 houses) and the Roche's Buildings in 1892 (128 houses). All of these buildings are still lived in by a new generation of Corkonians.

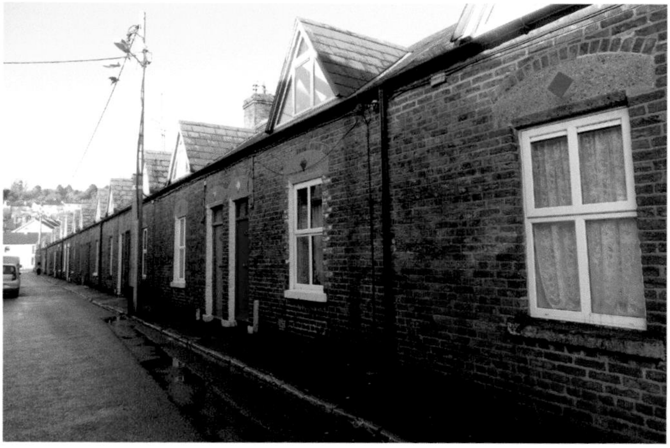

Madden's Buildings.

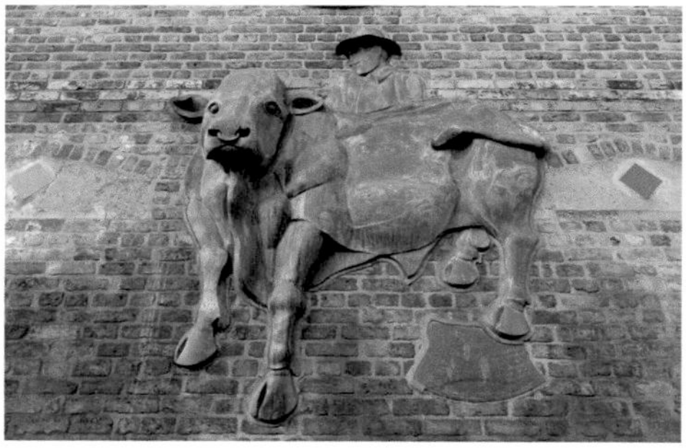

The 1993 sculpture on Madden's Buildings, Blackpool, signifying a former cattle market site.

39

Witness to Murder – The Tomás MacCurtain Memorial

Erected in 1999 with a design by Tighe O'Donoghue, the Tomás MacCurtain Memorial remembers Cork's Lord Mayor. Tomás was born on 20 March 1884 in a farmhouse in Ballyknockane townland, 14 miles north of Cork City. Tomás was the twelfth and last child of Patrick Curtin and Julia Sheehan. He was educated at the Burnfoot National School and later at the North Monastery School in Cork City.

Tomás MacCurtain, joined the Gaelic League in Blackpool, Cork City in 1901. By 1902 he was the group's secretary. Tomás had a very attentive memory, loved Irish poetry, music and dancing. He was very interested in Irish history and archaeology and learnt to play the bagpipes. He was an accomplished violin player and sometimes played in an orchestra. This brown-haired, blue-eyed Irishman had great determination and business capacity.

At the age of thirteen, in 1897, Tomás moved to the city to live with his sister at No. 68 Great Britain Street and attended the Christian Brothers North Monastery where he began to learn Irish. After Tomás left school he worked as a Clerk for the City of Cork Steam Packet Company. In 1907 he secured work at Marks Mills in Crosses Green and in his spare time he taught the Gaelic language to those wishing to learn.

By 1911, Tomás was involved in the running of Fianna Eireann, and became a Volunteer in 1914. He wanted to see a revival of the Irish language and national freedom and for his cause he served prison terms in 1916 and 1917 in Wakefield, Frongoch and Reading in England.

Tomás met Eilis Walsh, daughter of stonemason John Walsh. She was very active in the Gaelic League and they married on 28 June 1908. They had six children, the first dying as an infant – Patrick, Siobhan, Sile, Maura, Eilis and Thomas Jr. They made their home at No. 40 Thomas Davis Street, Blackpool, in the northern part of Cork City.

In January 1920, local government elections were held in Cork City, and Sinn Féin got the opportunity of dominating local councils. Tomás was elected by the people of his ward, N-W No. 3, and was selected to be the Lord Mayor of Cork City.

Just after 1 a.m. on Saturday 20 March 1920, men with blackened faces and in semi-disguise burst into the MacCurtain home. They knew their way to the main bedroom. They were from the Royal Irish Constabulary and shot the Lord Mayor.

In the house at the time were Mrs MacCurtain and her five children, plus her brother (James Walsh), three sisters, two nieces, a nephew and the elderly Mrs Walsh. Tomás died from shock and haemorrhage caused by bullet wounds and passed away after receiving the last rites.

Public reaction was significant and so a large funeral was held on Monday 22 March, from the North Cathedral. He was laid to rest in St Finbarr's Church graveyard, in a plot facing the main gate.

As the news got out into the public realm after the murder of Tomás MacCurtain, it sent shockwaves throughout every household – he had been Lord Mayor for less than fifty days and was just thirty-six years old. People began to discuss their relationship with Tomás within Cork City. Some revered his character and work. Others saw his work as another part of the way of life of a busy port city, which had many activities happening on any given day. But for a time, his murder brought Cork and the region to a standstill. This was another intensification of all-out war held across the streets of Cork that in time would be named the Irish War of Independence.

An outpouring of public grief was heard in speeches in the following days. In the weeks that followed the public inquest of his death revealed more questions than answers as to who actually killed him.

The verdict proposed that it was a government and RIC cover up, but unfortunately no official statement has ever come forward.

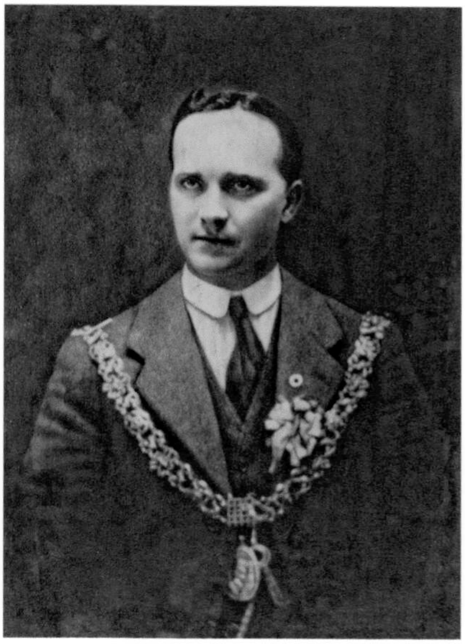

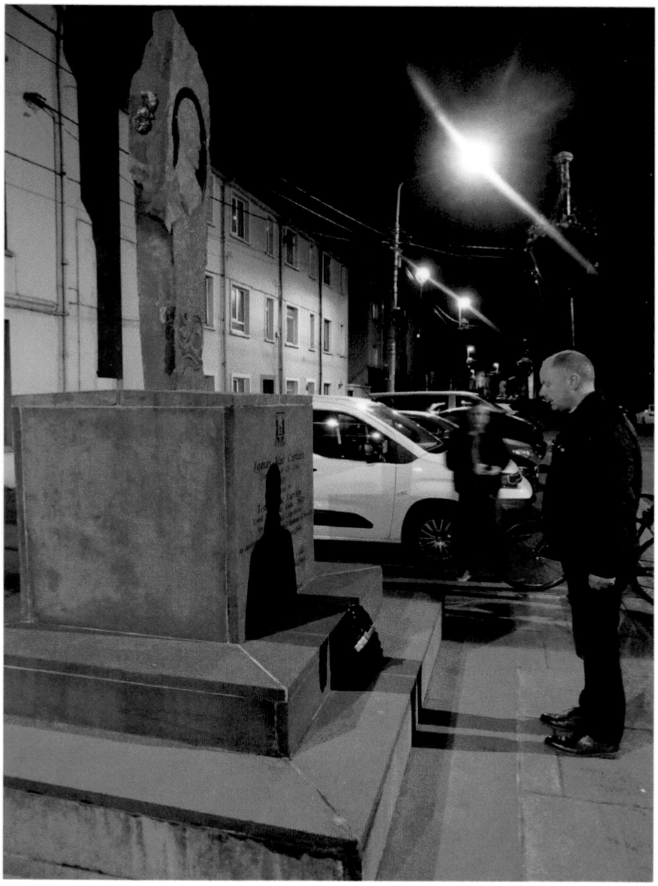

Above: Lord Mayor Alderman Tomás MacCurtain on his mayoral election night, 30 January 1920. (Courtesy of Cork City Council)

Right: Centenary commemoration on the morning of 20 March 2022 with Councillor Mick Nugent at Tighe O'Donoghue's MacCurtain memorial on Thomas Davis Street.

40

Church of the Annunciation

The Church of the Annunciation on Great William O'Brien Street in Blackpool replaced an earlier church called St Nicholas (built 1895), which was officially dedicated on 7 October 1945. Its design was by the noted Blackpool stone carver Seamus Murphy. The church was built by the staff of Sunbeam Wolsey (under Mick Callaghan, foreman) of which Mr William Dwyer was the founder and managing director.

Seamus Murphy, a native of Mallow, had a stone yard on Watercourse Road for many years. Other well-known works by Murphy include the bust of Michael Collins in Fitzgerald's Park, the busts of Seán Ó Faoláin and Frank O'Connor in the Cork City Library and the curious little water trough for dogs on St Patrick's Street.

The church was designed and built as a replacement for St Nicholas' Church, which stood on the site. St Nicholas' was constructed in 1895 by adapting the Blackpool National

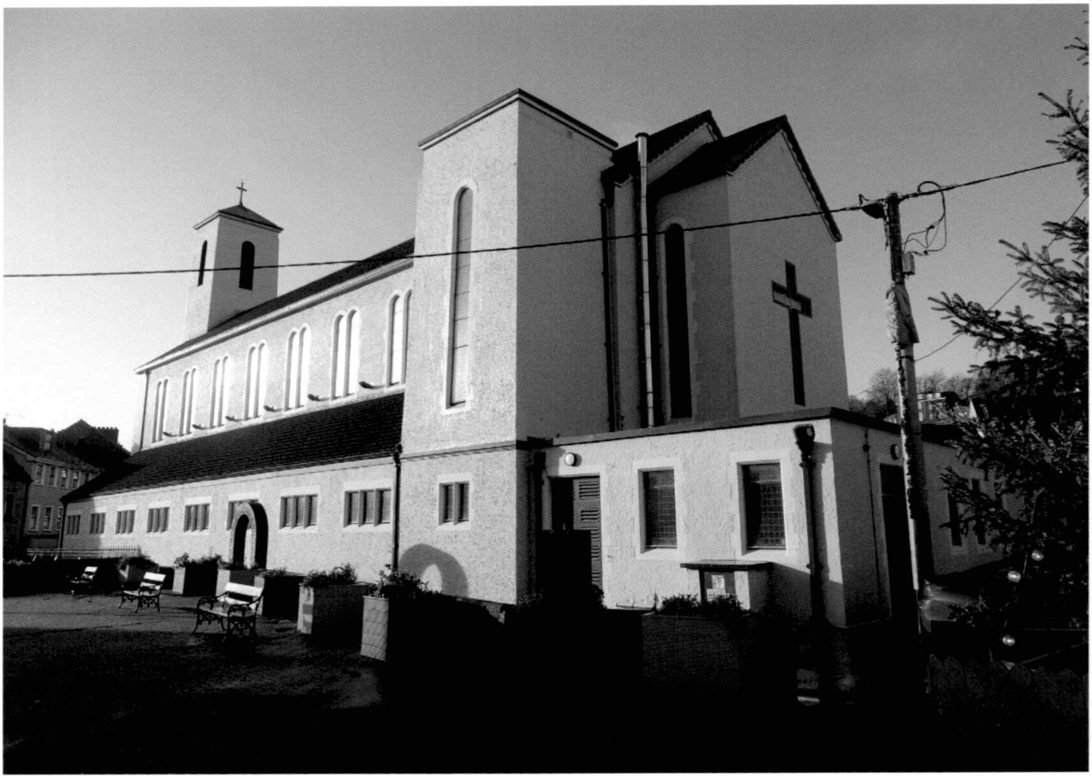

Church of the Annunciation on Great William O'Brien Street, Blackpool.

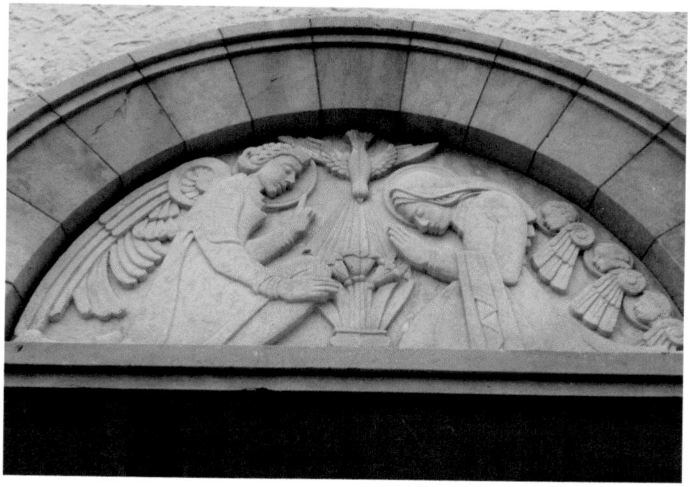

Annunciation panel by Seamus Murphy at the entrance of the Church of the Annunciation, Blackpool.

School building, which then moved to Brockelsby Street. It was financed by Nicholas Murphy of Blarney Woollen Mills. A police barracks had also occupied part of the site.

The Church of the Annunciation is constructed of concrete blocks, stipple plastered inside and out. There is an 80-foot bell tower and two smaller towers that form the transepts. The stained glass, including the impressive crucifix, sanctuary windows and the picture gallery of Our Lord (nave windows), are by Harry Clarke Studios in Dublin.

The tabernacle, lamp, candlesticks and other brasses were designed by Seamus Murphy and made by Gunnings in Dublin.

The stonework in the church is mostly by Murphy himself. His works include: the Annunciation panel over the front door, the Annunciation tablet on the exterior side wall, the Dwyer Plaque in the porch, the baptismal font originally at rear of the church and now near the altar, the holy water fonts in polished black limestone, the main altar depicting corn and grapes, the children's altar depicting the holy family, and Our Lady's altar depicting a crowned angel and foliage.

The most striking stonework in the church includes the Madonna and Sacred Heart statues on either side of the main altar. The Sacred Heart is in Portland stone with a marble base and was added to the church in 1947. It is 6 feet high. The Madonna was in the church in 1945 but was located on Our Lady's altar. It has subsequently been moved to its present position. It is 5 feet 6 inches high and is signed 'Seamus Murphy 45'.

41

Lido Cinema

Blackpool Cinema first opened on the site in 1920 and was reopened as the Lido in 1931 following renovations. It closed in the early 1960s following a stabbing incident and reopened as the Palladium for a short time, before closing for good in 1965.

Local historian Tom Foley remembers has vivid memories of the role the local Lido cinema played in the lives of children growing up in the area in the 1940s and 1950s:

> You could pay to get into the cinema with jam jars. You could get a ha'penny each for a jam jar, and it was fourpence to get into the Lido. When they'd start the projector, it took extra electricity and so the exit lights would dim. That's how we knew the picture was going to come on. There were wooden seats in the front and padded seats that cost a shilling in the back; when the lights went down, five or six would hop over into

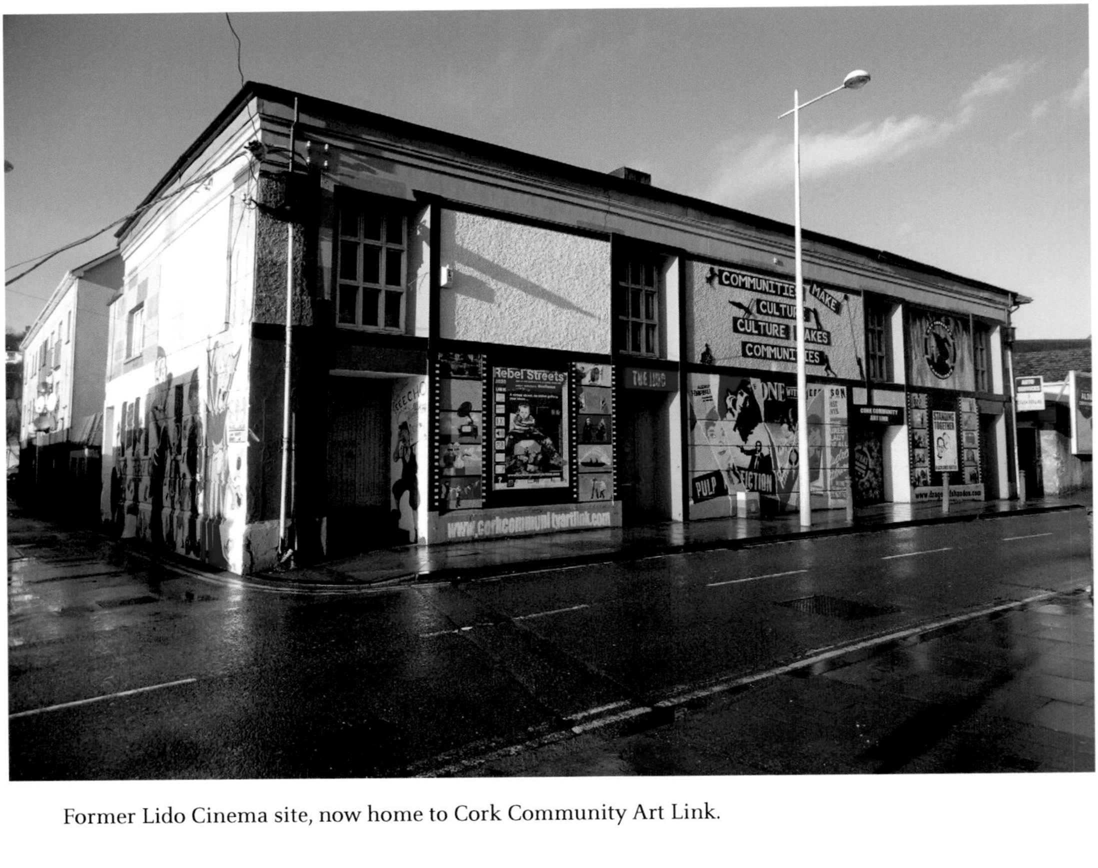

Former Lido Cinema site, now home to Cork Community Art Link.

> the padded seats and the manager, a Mr Coughlan, would have to come down with his flashlamp to try to get them out.
>
> There'd be three films on a week, and it cost the same to go in to the three in the Lido as it cost to go into the Savoy in town once. Most of our teenage years were spent going to the Lido three times a week.
>
> Running messages for elderly neighbours was one way of earning the entrance fee, and another was to collect empty jam jars, eight of which would cover the price of a ticket.

After its cinema days, the building housed O'Meara's camping supplies shop for many years. It is now home to Cork Community Art Link (CCAL).

From St Patrick's Day and Bonfire Night in Cork's Middle Parish in the 1990s to the Dragon of Shandon, Cork Community Artlink (CCAL) works in partnership with people to co-create, celebrate and imagine together. Its website emphasises that each street spectacle project undertaken by CCAL is based on an extensive outreach programme in partnership with the community and voluntary sector.

High standards of artistic excellence are encouraged, as is the researching of new techniques and ways of making unique puppets and props. Voluntary participation is the foundation of each project with lots of opportunities for adults to come along, learn new skills and make a creative contribution to the community.

42

Hewitt's Distillery

Hewitt's Watercourse Distillery was established in 1792 by Thomas Hewitt, John Teulon (both butter merchants) and Richard Blunt (a London distiller). By 1794 the production and sale of whiskey had begun.

Although sales kept rising during the first decade of the nineteenth century, the distillery was having endless trouble with water power due to the many other industrial concerns using the same supply. Consequently in 1811 the company purchased two steam engines (a new technology) from Birmingham at a cost of £2,062.

The Watercourse Distillery was one of the first distilleries in the country to do so. The company even bought a large sawmill in 1830, which they subsequently dismantled so that there would be one less claim to the millrace and hence the limited supply of water.

The distilleries in the Cork harbour area primarily produced pot still whiskey (repeated distillations producing a spirit with a characteristic flavour), but by the early 1830s patent or continuous stills (more economical and producing spirits with a higher alcohol content but with less flavour) were employed at the Watercourse Distillery.

In 1834 the Hewitt family took sole ownership of the distillery, and a full description of it was drawn up at the time for insurance purposes. The building inventory included a boiler and still house, containing three iron steam boilers; a brewhouse, which also contained boilers and cast-metal mash tuns; a fermenting back house with coolers; two

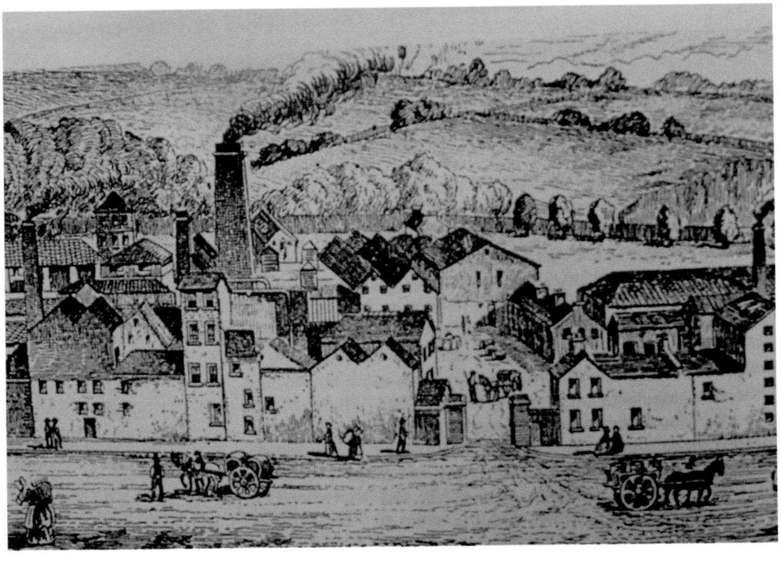

Sketch of Hewitt's Watercourse Distillery, 1869. (Courtesy of Cork City Library)

engine houses with a number of boilers (with three steam engines); a malthouse; kilns; a corn store; spirit store; and watermills.

The Hewitt family sold the distillery to the Cork Distillers Company in 1868. By 1876, distilling had ceased at the Watercourse Distillery, although the maltings, corn stores and warehouses were still used by the company.

According to local information this latter building was used for yeast fermenting and drying during the 1940s and 1950s. By this time the distilling process had been relocated to the North Mall Distillery and Irish Distillers Ltd used the majority of the buildings at the Watercourse Road complex solely as warehouses. A cooperage was still in business, however, and occupied a workshop in the southern area of the industrial estate.

Following the demolition of some industrial buildings for the construction of the bypass of Blackpool village (which began in February 1997) the ground plan of several early nineteenth-century buildings were uncovered and recorded during archaeological monitoring of the construction works by a team of archaeologists from Cork City Council. One of these sites was part of Hewitt's Watercourse Distillery (the Steam Mills/Grain Store Building), which were dated to the end of the eighteenth century/the beginning of the nineteenth century.

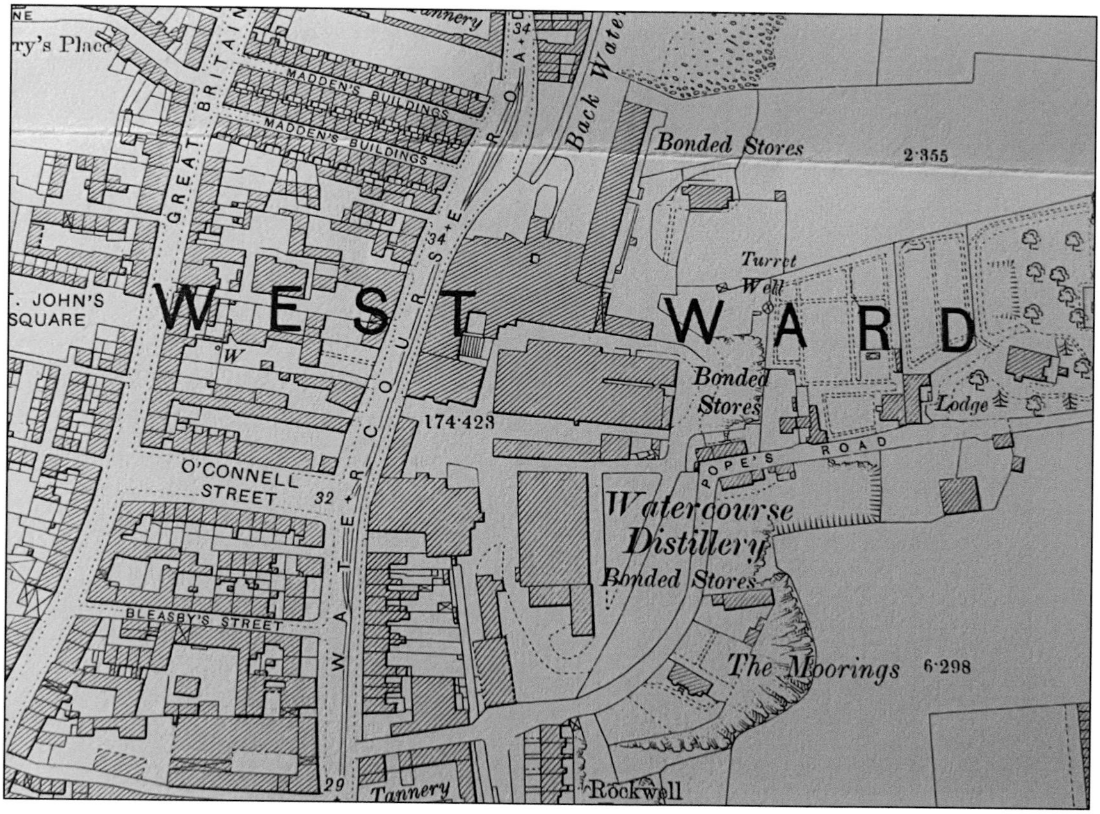

Map of Hewitt's Watercourse Distillery, 1900. (Courtesy of Cork City Library)

43

Blackpool and Its Tanneries

Blackpool was the scene of industry in Cork in the eighteenth and nineteenth centuries. In this district various attempts were made at various times to start or revive the manufacture of textiles such as broadcloth, blankets, flannels, hosiery, thread, braid and rope.

The leather industry was also vibrant in the Blackpool area, giving employment to over 700 hands and tanning on average 110,000 hides annually.

Tanning is the process of making leather (which does not easily decompose) from the skins of animals (which do). Traditionally, tanning used tannin, an acidic chemical compound. Colouring may occur during tanning. A tannery is the term for a place where these skins are processed.

In 1835, records of industrial enterprises reveal that there were possibly forty-six tan yards in different parts of the city, the most extensive being located in the North Gate Bridge vicinity where there were 615 tanners in constant employment. The average

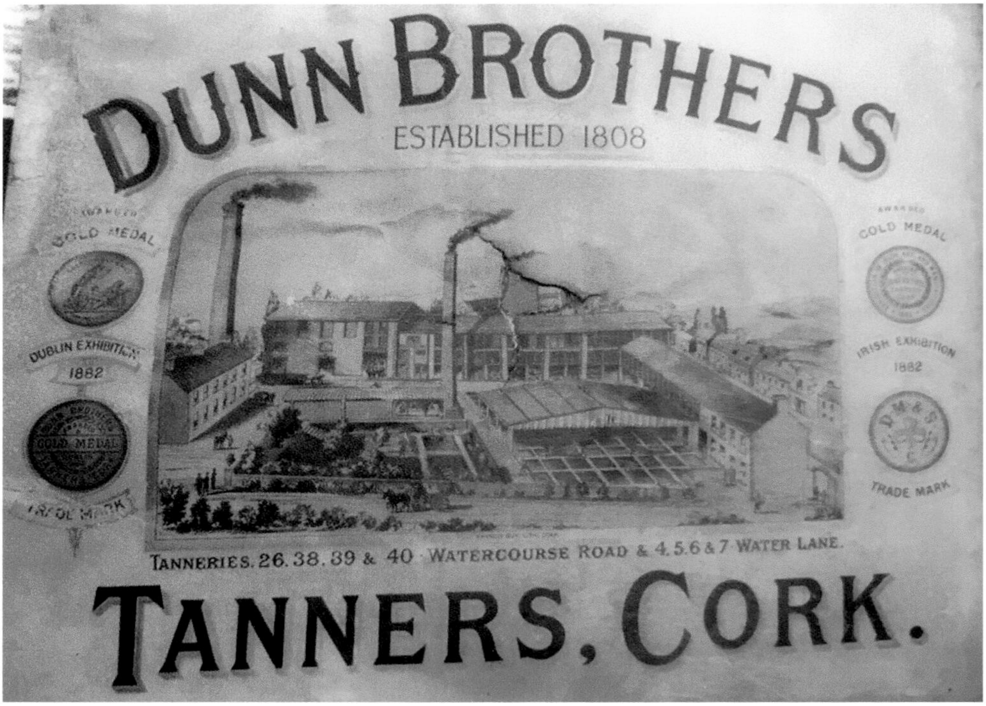

Advertisement for Dunn's Tannery, Watercourse Road, late nineteenth century. (Courtesy of Cork City Library)

number of hides tanned annually amounted to 110,000 and from 1835 onwards tanners found it necessary to import hides from as far afield as Montevideo and Gibraltar in order to supplement local supplies.

Richard Griffith's evaluation of 1852 listed twenty-one tanneries in the Blackpool area. By the turn of the twentieth century only a handful of tanneries remained in production. The main tannery was Dunn's on the Watercourse Road.

One of the most extensive tan yards in Cork belonged to Daniel, fourth son of Jeremiah Murphy. This was located in Blackpool. The firm of Daniel Murphy & Sons was not affected by the decline, which ruined many tanning enterprises following the 1830s. A partnership formed with the firm of Dunn Brothers maintained the business and the new firm became the largest tanning concern in the country at the time. The Great Famine dealt the industry a very serious blow from which it never recovered. From that date onwards, the industry steadily declined.

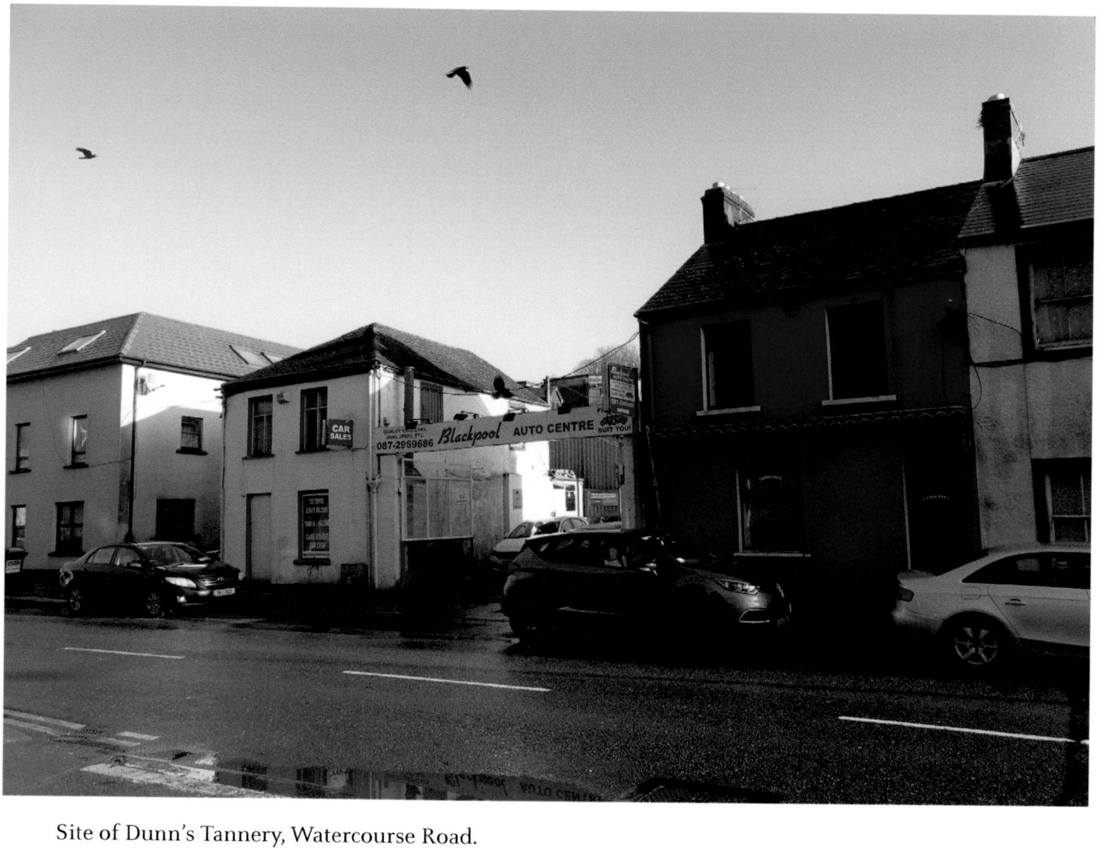

Site of Dunn's Tannery, Watercourse Road.

The Foundling Hospital

The Foundling Hospital for Cork's impoverished children was established at Leitrim Street in 1747 on a site now occupied by Heineken Ireland. It is argued by historians that the inside of the brewery's old entrance arch is part of the old entrance to the old Foundling Hospital.

On a map by John Rocque of Cork in 1759 it is marked as the poorhouse. It was mainly funded by a tax on the import of coal. Samuel Lewis wrote in 1837 that the building was a small quadrangle, of which the chapel formed one side and the other three were appropriated to schoolrooms (two for the boys and two for the girls), dormitories and other necessary apartments. Lewis further details that the hospital was governed by an incorporated board consisting of the diocesan, mayor, recorder, aldermen, sheriffs, common councilmen and a common speaker. Lewis describes that the infants received periodically from the churchwardens were placed out at nurse till they were six or seven years old, when they became inmates until of an age to be apprenticed. The average number of the former nursed children was 1,000. Of the latter children to be apprenticed, they were educated as Protestant and bound to Protestant masters.

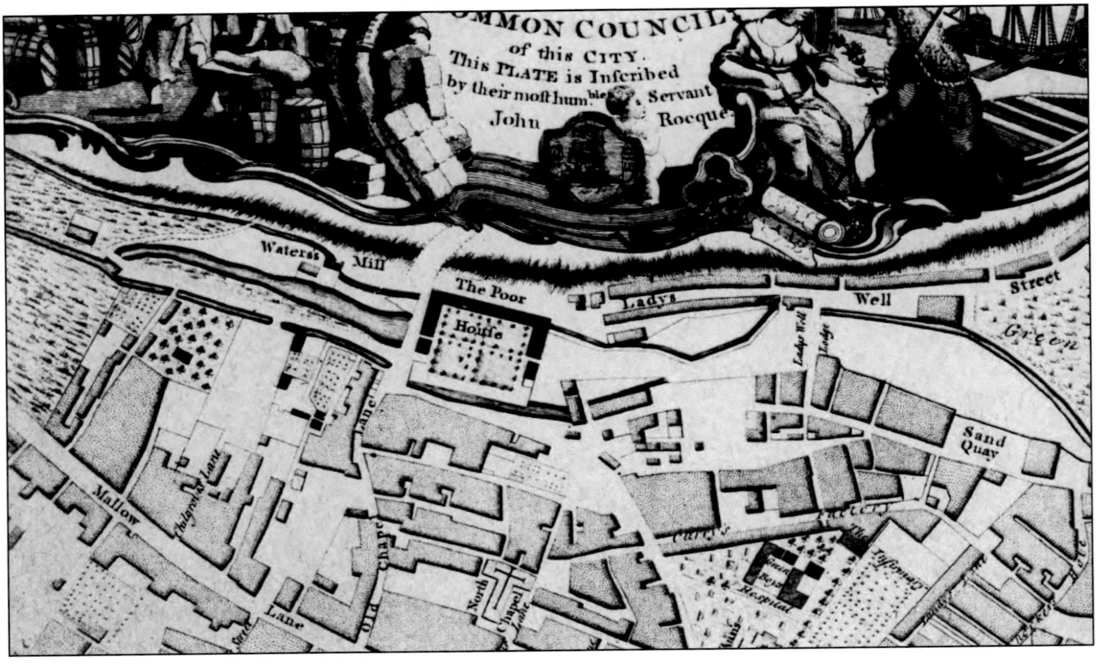

Cork Poor House as depicted on John Rocque's Map of Cork, *c.* 1759. (Courtesy of Cork City Library)

The governors of the hospital sanctioned a resolution in 1838 that no new admissions would be permitted and the numbers, therefore, declined until there were but sixteen. Two years later the buildings were sold for £1,200 by the Poor Law Commissioners and the money was placed to the credit of the Cork Board of Guardians. The inmates were transferred to the Cork Workhouse on Cork's Douglas Road.

Now the home of Heineken Ireland, its predecessor Our Lady's Well Brewery was founded on the Foundling Hospital site in 1854 by James J., William J., Jerome and Francis J. Murphy. In 1884, the business was transformed into a private limited company, of which Francis Murphy was chairman.

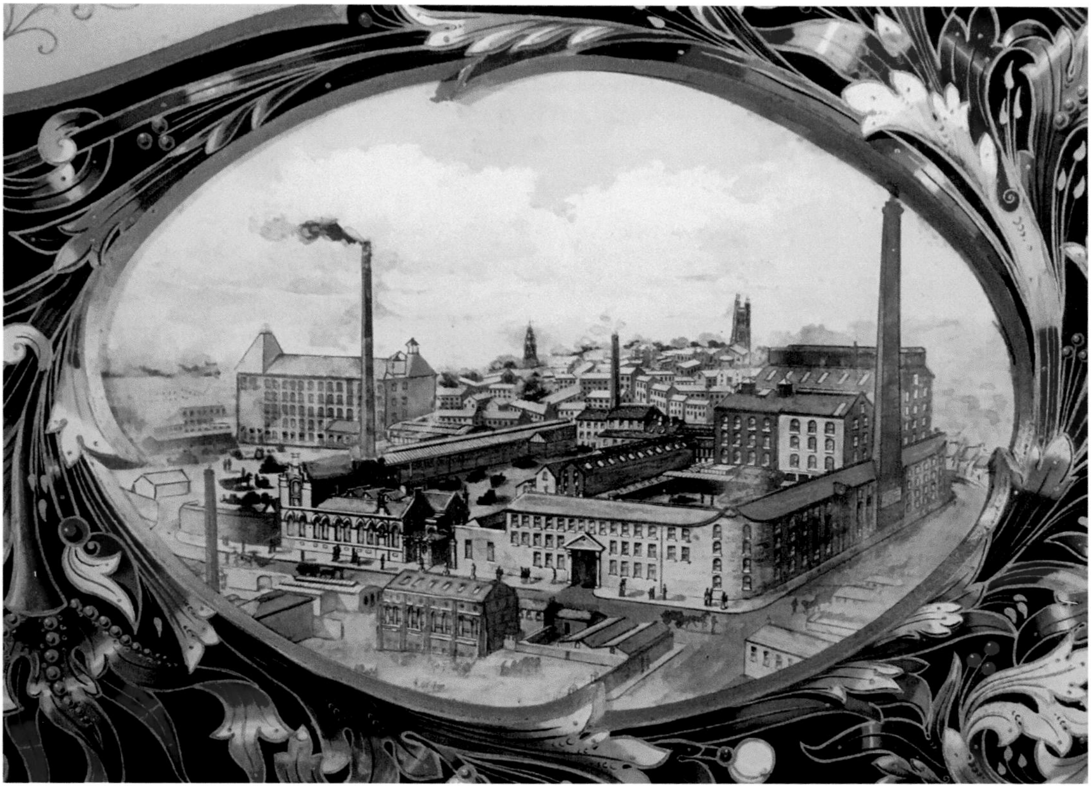

Postcard of Our Lady's Well Brewery, Blackpool, *c.* 1900. (Courtesy of Cork Public Museum)

45

Atop Fever Hospital Steps

The Fever Hospital had a distinguished career caring for Corkonians since 1802, located atop the steps adjacent Our Lady's Well in Blackpool. It was founded by Corkman Dr Milner Barry, who introduced vaccination into Cork in 1800 and was the first to make it known to any Irish city. In 1824, a monument with a long laudatory inscription was erected in his memory in the grounds of the Fever Hospital by Corkonians.

An annual general meeting of the president and assistants of the Cork Fever Hospital and House of Recovery was held on 15 May 1917 in the Crawford Municipal School of Art. The annual report of the Hospital Committee was read by member Sir John Scott. He revealed that on 1 January 1917 there were thirty-seven patients in the hospital and 256 were admitted during 1916. This made a total number of 293 patients treated, compared with 500 during the year 1915. Of the patients treated, 253 were discharged and cured while eleven remained in hospital on 31 December 1916. There were twenty-four deaths during the year, and it was noted, with great regret, that many of them were only brought to the hospital in a 'hopeless condition'. Deducting these from the number of deaths, the mortality showed a low rate of 6 per cent, which was deemed by the committee as a 'satisfactory outcome' with dealing with dangerous life-taking fevers.

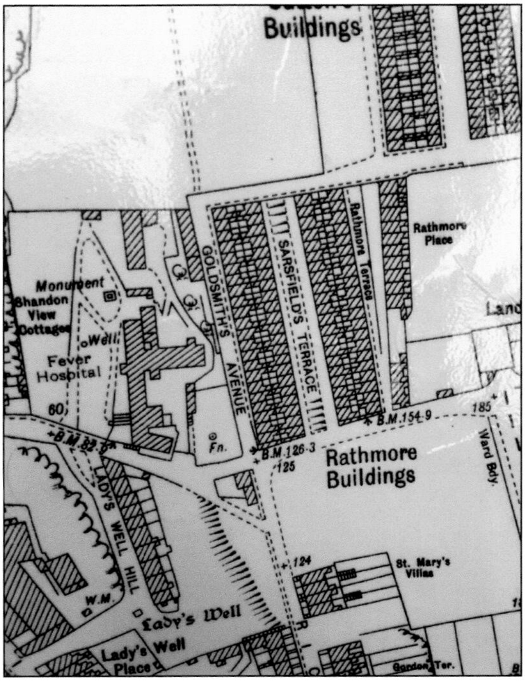

The site of Fever Hospital on the 1949 Ordnance Survey Map. (Courtesy of Cork City Library)

A regular call was made by the Fever Hospital urging upon Cork citizens the immense importance of prompt isolation and hospital treatment for cases of infectious diseases. Many of the cases treated came from the thickly populated districts the city. Of the cases admitted, 108 came from the north side of the city, fifty-four from the south side, fifty-three from the centre and twenty-five from the rural districts.

A considerable number of military cases were treated. One soldier, having returned to his home in England, wrote a letter to Dr Sutton, the resident medical officer, thanking him and the medical staff for the 'excellent treatment' he had received. He stated he had been in hospitals in various parts of the world but that he never got better care and attention than he received in the Cork Fever Hospital under Dr Sutton and Miss McCullagh, the matron.

The committee regretted to report that a case of typhus fever was admitted to the hospital from a Cork locality. It was some years since there had been a case of typhus fever in Cork, mainly owing to the excellent and watchful eye of the officials of the Public Health Department of Cork Corporation. They were active in their endeavours to promote cleanliness and to guard against overcrowding in congested areas, thus prevent the outbreak and spread of any infectious diseases.

In the report of the medical staff, read by Dr O'Callaghan, he called upon parents and guardians of unvaccinated children – a substantial number of whom were in the city – to have them immediately vaccinated as there was every danger that smallpox might be brought into the country by some of those returning from the various fronts of the war. It was hoped that the Board of Guardians, who were responsible for the enforcement of the Vaccination Act, would insist on it being complied with by parents and others in charge of children. Under the amended 1907 Act the parent could escape penalties for the non-vaccination of their child if within four months from the birth they made a statutory declaration that they confidently believed vaccination would be prejudicial to the health of the child.

The high cost of living meant the Fever Hospital was considerably expensive to maintain. It was acknowledged that the cost of treating fever patients was heavy. The increase in prices was shown by a comparative return made by the auditor, who pointed out that in the year 1913, before the war, the cost of food and necessaries amounted to £416 14*s* 7*d*. During 1916–17 the cost under the same headings came to £850 8*s* 2*d* – a rise of over 101 per cent.

The hospital site was sold off in 1962 and the housing estate of Shandon Court now stands in its stead.

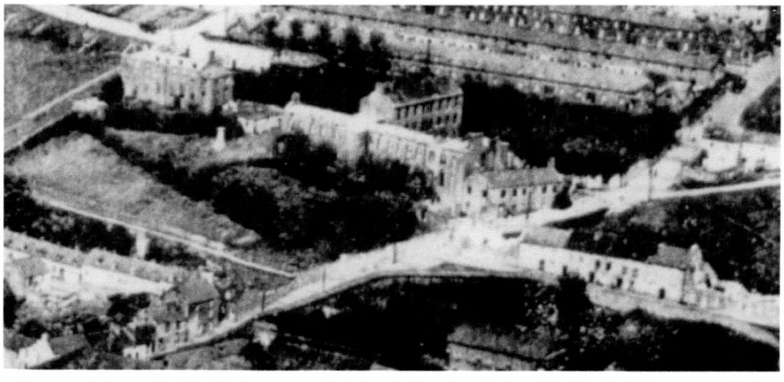

Fever Hospital, Cork, *c*. 1930. (Courtesy of Cork City Library)

46

Views of Cork at Audley Place

When the Corporation of Cork invested in the planning St Patrick's Bridge in 1787, it opened up a new quarter for development. The 1790s saw the creation of St Patrick's Hill – an avenue from Bridge Street that aligned with an old windmill now incorporated into Audley House. This decade also saw the creation of an early MacCurtain Street – back then known as Strand Street and later King Street, then Summerhill North from 1820 onwards.

Over the centuries, artists, travellers and antiquarians have tried to capture the essence of St Patrick's Hill and the vista from Audley Place. In more recent times, the view was captured by producers of *The Young Offenders* as its two main characters, Jock and Connor, chat about their lives on a bench.

Ascent has always been difficult for any mode of transport, from horse and cart to cars. In 1988, the organisers of the Tour de France held a section of their race in Ireland and sent their competitors on a gruelling assent of St Patrick's Hill. There is a spectacular view of the city at the top, especially of the northside suburbs of Blackpool, Gurrananbraher and northwards to Knocknaheeny and Farranree. The river can also be seen winding its way through the city, on its way to meet the waters of the Atlantic Ocean.

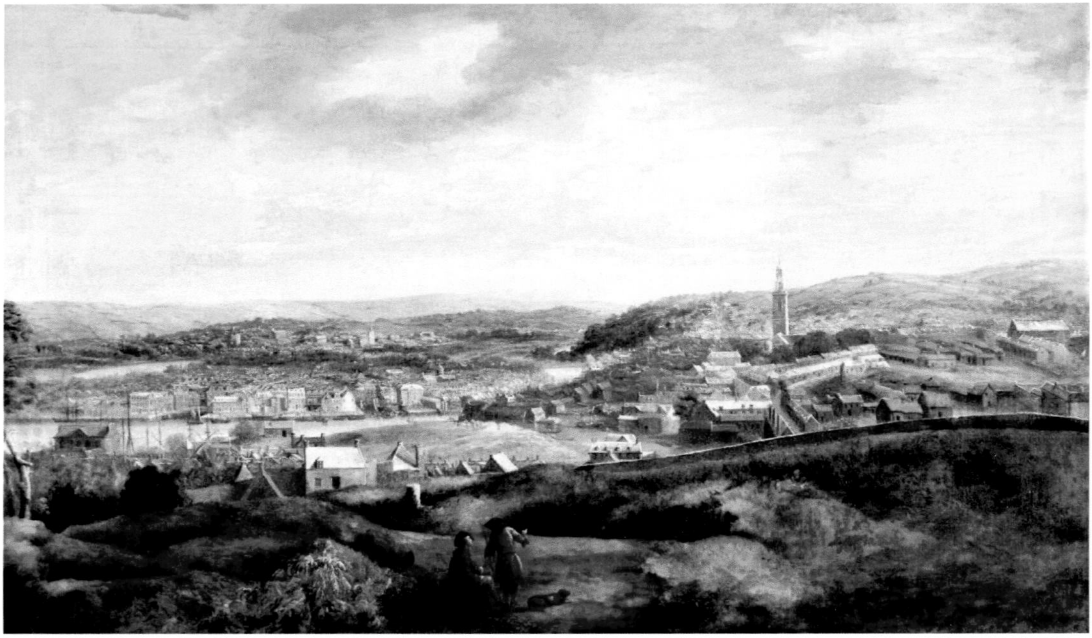

View of Cork by John Butts, 1760. (Courtesy of Crawford Art Gallery)

The origins of the name Audley Place or Bell's Field have been lost to time. Bell's Field may be a reference to a Major Bell who may have been connected to what is now nearby Collins Barracks.

This view from the top is much loved and often photographed. It has been captured through numerous mediums: a sketch by historian Charles Smith in 1750, a painting by John Butts in the 1760s (now on display in the Crawford Art Gallery) and photographic postcards in the early nineteenth century among others. The early depictions show the early growth of Blackpool as an industrial hub in the city with its myriad of chimneys reflecting the many tanneries and distilleries in the area. Many of these were established in the late eighteenth century.

St Anne's Shandon, with its ornate steeple, dominates all sketches and photographs. The tower is very symbolic of eighteenth-century expansion in Cork. The adjacent butter market, located off Shandon Street, remembers the golden age of prosperity and profit in the city.

A postcard from *c.* 1890 shows the minarets of St Mary's and St Anne's North Cathedral and echoes the social and physical change of nineteenth-century Victorian Cork. Just to the top of the early nineteenth-century photograph are farmed green fields, which were developed with housing estates in the early 1930s, a testament to the growing population of a city and a way to ease the slum conditions of the inner city. Today, standing at the spot of the viewer, one can see the suburban growth in Knocknaheeny and further east in Farranree.

Cork City Council are trying to encourage the recreational use of the area of the top of the hill by supplying seating and landscaping the general area.

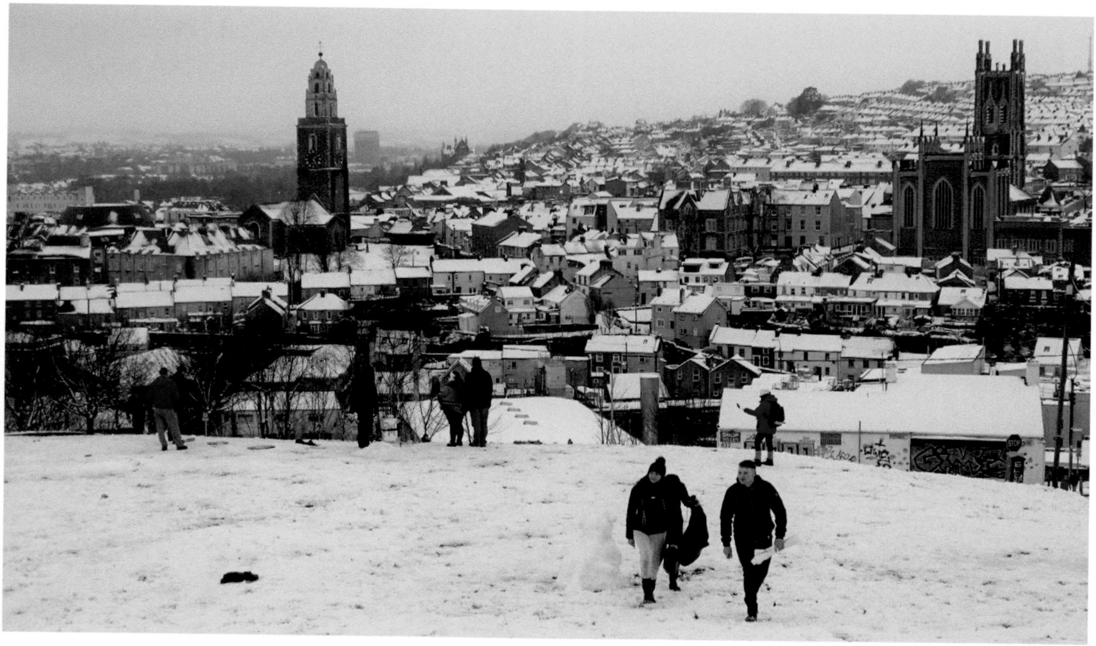

View from Audley Place on a snowy day, March 2018.

Acknowledgements

I would like to sincerely thank the commissioning and editorial staff at Amberley Publishing for continuing to put their faith in my books and for the valuable advice and assistance they always provide. I would like to express my gratitude to my parents, my family and the supportive public for continually pushing me to explore, think and write about Cork city, its region and their cultural heritage.

About the Author

For thirty years Kieran McCarthy has actively promoted Cork's heritage, its various communities and people. He has led and continues to lead successful heritage initiatives through his community talks, city school heritage programmes, walking tours, newspaper articles, books and his work through his heritage consultancy business. For the past twenty-five years, Kieran has written a local heritage column in the *Cork Independent* on the history, geography and its intersection with modern-day life in communities in Cork City and County. Kieran is the author of thirty local history books. He holds a PhD in Geography from the National University of Ireland and has interests in ideas of landscape, collective memory, narrative and identity structures. In June 2009, May 2014 and May 2019 Kieran was elected as a local government councillor (Independent) to Cork City Council. He is also a member of the European Committee of the Regions. In 2023–24, Kieran was Lord Mayor of Cork. More on Kieran's work can be viewed at www.corkheritage.ie and www.kieranmccarthy.ie.

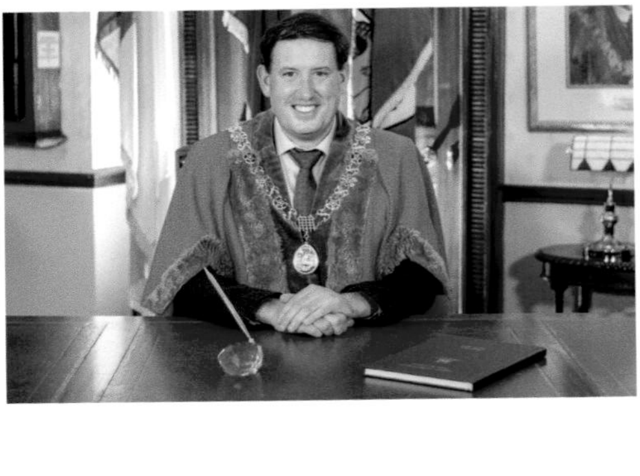